The Meat and Potatoes of Life

My True Lit Com

LISA SMITH MOLINARI

Elva Resa ∗ Saint Paul

The Meat and Potatoes of Life: My True Lit Com
©2020 Lisa Smith Molinari

This book is a memoir, reflecting the author's recollection of actual events. Every effort has been made to tell the truth, the whole truth, and sometimes an exaggerated version of the truth. Some names have been changed to protect the innocent and the guilty.

Front cover illustration, hand lettering, and book design by Jessie Barnes for Elva Resa. Senior editor Terri Barnes.

Library of Congress Cataloging-in-Publication Data

Names: Molinari, Lisa Smith, 1966- author.
Title: The meat and potatoes of life : my true lit com / Lisa Smith Molinari.
Description: Saint Paul : Elva Resa, [2020] | Summary: "Humorous memoir of an attorney who leaves her law career to become a navy wife and stay at home mom of three…"-- Provided by publisher.
Identifiers: LCCN 2019049231 (print) | LCCN 2019049232 (ebook) | ISBN 9781934617540 (hardcover) | ISBN 9781934617557 (epub) | ISBN 9781934617564 (kindle edition)
Subjects: LCSH: Military spouses--United States--Social conditions. | Navy spouses--United States--Anecdotes. | United States. Navy--Military life--Anecdotes. | Military spouses--United States--Anecdotes. | Children of military personnel--United States--Anecdotes.
Classification: LCC UB403 .M65 2020 (print) | LCC UB403 (ebook) | DDC 359.1/20973--dc23
LC record available at https://lccn.loc.gov/2019049231
LC ebook record available at https://lccn.loc.gov/2019049232

Printed in United States of America.
10 9 8 7 6 5 4 3 2 1

Published by
Elva Resa Publishing
8362 Tamarack Vlg., Ste. 119-106
St. Paul, MN 55125

ElvaResa.com
MilitaryFamilyBooks.com
Bulk discounts available.

For Hayden, Anna, and Lilly.
I love you more than life itself.

Now go empty the dishwasher.

CONTENTS

Season Three | In the Trenches ~ 83

Season Four | In It to Win It ~ 135

A WORD FROM
OUR SPONSOR

My family life reminds me of a television sitcom. Although the script does not follow a three-act formula, we don't take commercial breaks, and there is no studio audience, we do have scenes and subplots, heroes and anti-heroes, problems, solutions, and plenty of comic relief. Unlike sitcoms that end with a heartwarming or hilarious message, the meaning in my reality is not always clear. It often gets muddled with the trivial, mundane, and chaotic details in my daily routine. I have to peel away the layers to find my own hidden story arc.

These are the stories that helped me stay afloat over the last decade.

Each season represents an era in our family life, starting with marriage and progressing from the honeymoon to changing diapers, pee-wee soccer to itemizing deductions, middle school dances to driver's permits, summer vacations to sassy teenagers, college visits to an empty nest.

Each episode involves the same cast of eccentric characters: The lovable husband who doesn't know the difference between a flat-head and a Phillips screwdriver. The harried mom who hides an emergency can of Pringles in the laundry room. The quirky son who gives one-word answers to every question. The fashion-conscious daughter who milks her victimization as the middle child. The fun-loving youngest child who lives on social media. And the family dog, the only one who seems to have it all figured out.

Our perspective as a navy family also makes frequent appearances, adding another dimension to experiences and events common to many families.

So grab some kettle corn and a bottle of cheap pinot noir—they pair well, I promise—snuggle up on the couch, and get ready to laugh, cry, and rediscover the meaning hidden in the madness of modern family life.

THE RISE AND FALL
OF SUPERMOM

Life was so much simpler when I was a kid.

I didn't wake up in the morning worrying about social media profiles, glycemic indexes, or incandescent bulbs. I thumped out of bed, blissfully ignorant that my polyester nightgown was highly-flammable. I removed the faux-denim strap of my orthodontic headgear before padding off to the kitchen for a bowl of Cap'n Crunch or non-free-range eggs with buttered Wonder Bread, washed down with Donald Duck orange juice from a can.

Over breakfast, I wondered what the day might bring.

Would Mom agree to drop me off at the pool if I waited until she was done sunbathing in the back yard in her rollers? Would the kid next door want to come over to play, or was there still a beehive in the metal tube of our swing set? Would Dad let me ride my banana-seat Schwinn into town if I promised to pick him up a pack of Salems from the pull-lever cigarette machine in the Capitol Diner on the way home?

My biggest worry was whether my older brother, Tray, and his trouble-making friends would chase me around the neighborhood again with dog poop speared on a stick.

As a teen, I slogged through school gauging my enjoyment of each day by such mundane triumphs as staying awake in geometry class and finding peanut butter bars on the cafeteria lunch menu. At night, I talked to my best friend, Patti, for hours on my bedroom telephone, sorting out our insecurities and dreaming of being popular. On weekends, we'd sneak into the local drive-in theater, walk around the mall slurping Orange Juliuses, or borrow her parents' station wagon to cruise past the local arcade in hopes the boys would stop playing *Asteroids* long enough to notice us.

Although I feared my lack of curling iron skills could potentially leave me without a boyfriend, I had no real worries other than a normal dose of teen angst.

Years later when I became a wife and mother, I began to wonder, *Why, after such a carefree upbringing, am I ridden with guilt over using plastic grocery bags or the wrong sugar substitute? Why does my eye twitch when I hear my smartphone message notifications? And why do I hyperventilate when the DVR reaches ninety-eight percent?*

Arguably, there comes a point when marriage, parenting, and family life in the twenty-first century takes more intelligence, physical energy, and organizational skills than most human beings possess.

I reached that tipping point long ago.

It was the late nineties. With three kids, our family life was hectic, but we were plodding along, happily keeping our heads above water.

My husband, Francis, and I bought a suburban Dutch colonial on a cul-de-sac, with an inviting little porch and a wooden play set. As a navy man, Francis worked long hours with frequent travel and occasional two- to six-month deployments, so I got used to taking charge of the kids, the household, and our sloppy 110-pound dog, Dinghy.

Of course, it wasn't easy managing the household alone, but I had given up my career as a litigation attorney to raise our family, and I was determined to do it right.

No matter what it took, I would be Supermom.

Even when we found out our oldest child, Hayden, had autism spectrum disorder, I did what needed to be done to keep the many gears of our family machine running smoothly, whether Francis was home or away.

Hayden's two younger sisters, Anna and Lilly, didn't understand "special needs." They grew up believing it was normal to play in therapists' waiting rooms for several hours each week, for their older brother to eat a strange diet, and for Mom to spend a lot of time with him in the playroom, jotting notes into a spiral-bound notebook throughout the day.

A slave to my routine, I woke each morning at six o'clock to get the kids up and dressed for school. I slurped coffee, packed lunches, and listened to AM radio while they ate Cheerios. After walking Hayden and Anna to the elementary school—one hand gripping a to-go cup and the other pushing Lilly in the stroller with a dog leash around my wrist—I'd rush back to drive Lilly to Montessori preschool in our minivan littered with Happy Meal toys and gummy bears. When I returned home, I had forty-five minutes to do laundry and make beds before my step aerobics class at the YMCA, followed by the preschool pick-up. My guilty pleasure was the half hour back at home, standing at the kitchen island, when I ate a turkey sandwich for lunch and watched *Days of Our Lives*.

I maintained the same rigid efficiency in the afternoons, bringing paperwork, toys, and snacks to occupational and speech therapy appointments and doing play therapy with Hayden in the finished room over our garage while dinner was in the oven. After baths and bedtime stories, I'd hit the couch. But even then, I was multitasking: journaling Hayden's progress in my notebook, sewing Halloween costumes out of sweatshirts and felt, folding laundry, and balancing the checkbook.

On weekends we rushed to soccer and flag football games,

packed for scout campouts, went to church, cut grass, raked leaves, and cleaned gutters. Our rewards were simple: lawn chairs in the driveway on Saturdays at dusk, drinking cold beers with our neighbors and telling stories while the kids chased fireflies and rode scooters.

Though I was spinning multiple plates in the air, I somehow managed to keep it all together.

Then, life got more complicated.

On September 11, 2001, I was in the shower of the YMCA women's locker room, crying. Right after my step aerobics class, a fellow navy spouse had told me about the destruction of the World Trade Center towers in New York City in a suspected terrorist attack. She and I both knew this event was not just everyday bad news. It was an instant crisis of massive death and destruction on American soil. The US would have to respond quickly and with force and keep a more vigilant watch to prevent more attacks. This would change our lives forever. I quickly retrieved the kids from nursery and preschool and rushed home to watch the horror play out on television.

Immediately, new missions were announced, and the military's operational tempo gained speed. Francis, a naval intelligence officer, spent longer hours at work. At home, his mind was always on the daily intelligence briefing he would give the next day. Subsequent jobs sent him on frequent travel assignments, twice to Iraq for short stints. The years following 9/11 added a new level of stress to our lives, but also a fresh sense of purpose and patriotism. I was thankful Francis was not on the front lines. Even though his time away from home had increased, he hadn't been asked to deploy for long periods like some of our friends.

But then one afternoon, Francis came home early. He sat at our kitchen table, looked down at the folded khaki garrison cap in his hands and broke the news. He was deploying.

In Francis's career field, this was surprising news. While aviators, surface warfare officers, submariners, and other members of the navy were often sent on deployments, intelligence officers compete with each other for the few deployment slots available to them during their time in the military. I say "compete," because deployments, necessary to national security, are also beneficial to the careers of military officers.

Francis had volunteered to be an IA, individual augmentee, on an anti-terrorism task force. For him, this meant stateside training in South Carolina and Rhode Island followed by a yearlong deployment to Djibouti, Africa, adjacent to Somalia, which was known then as a haven for terrorists.

Selfishly, what I heard was that while he was off training in the States, then deployed to some godforsaken combat zone for at least a year, I would have to handle everything at home. *Alone.*

Many of my friends at the time were naval aviators' wives who were used to successive deployments. Even they reacted to my deployment news with gasps. This was not comforting. "A whole year?!" they exclaimed. "Oh, girl. You better start stocking up on wine now."

They assured me life as I knew it would soon come to an end, and the only way for me to survive was to lower my standards enough to shamelessly wear pajama pants all day and let the kids eat Fruit Loops for dinner. They told me about the frequent crying, the rat's nest hairdos, the justified consumption of afternoon alcoholic beverages, and the shopping binges they creatively referred to as retail therapy.

But I wasn't buying it. I was different. I was Supermom. I had proven I could rise to any challenge.

Besides, I didn't depend on Francis the same way my friends depended on their husbands.

Francis is no ordinary man. Sure, he loves watching football as much as the next guy. There isn't a cured-pork product he'd turn down. He has more than his share of body hair. And, like most guys, he goes into that weird trance-like state with half-open eyes and spittle on his chin when a Victoria's Secret commercial comes on.

Unlike most men, however, Francis openly admits to having no mechanical skills. He refers to hardware stores as haunted houses and thinks the most useful tool is a handyman's telephone number. I've seen him squeal and swat at the air like a scared little girl at the sight of a marauding bee or horsefly. He loves white wine, cricket sweaters, scented candles, fancy coffee, and has an interesting penchant for collecting Polish pottery. And although his family called him "Frank" when he was a kid, he prefers the presumption of refinement and sensitivity that comes with being known as "Francis."

So, when my friends—who depended entirely on their husbands to fix a leaky sink, grill the steaks, aerate the lawn, or hook up the DVD player—told me how hard deployment would be, I didn't believe them. I was already used to handling many of the traditional "husband duties" by myself. I was ready to fulfill my obligation as a navy wife and wholeheartedly believed I'd make the best of it.

To prepare for Francis's prolonged absence, we bought a few things to help keep us connected while he was away: a new computer for us at home, a laptop for him, and new cell phones. I entered the world of social media, hoping all these avenues of communication would simplify our complicated situation.

Francis left for his deployment unceremoniously on an airplane. Frankly, as a sailor's wife, I felt a little ripped off. I wanted to doll the kids up in red, white, and blue, and wave tearfully from the pier as a grey ship shoved off with the band on deck playing "Anchors Aweigh."

No such luck. After hugs and kisses next to a bagel kiosk at the airport, we watched as he disappeared into the security screening line, carrying his backpack and a clear plastic baggie of shampoo and toothpaste.

At first, it was fun debunking what I believed to be the myth of the beleaguered military spouse. I enjoyed not having to put a decent meal on the table for Francis. *Why cook a roast when the kids prefer boxed macaroni and cheese anyway?* And I was perfectly happy eating the remnants scraped out of the pot with a wooden spoon while standing over the sink. Later, after I put the kids to bed, I quite liked not having to share the TV remote, surfing to my heart's content between morally bankrupt reality shows and second-rate suspense films.

I spoke to Francis once a week through a bad Skype connection, but we sent sweet, humorous, or heartfelt emails almost every day. And in an absence-makes-the-heart-grow-fonder kind of way, romance flourished, because we used our brief contact time to communicate that we didn't take each other for granted.

As for the kids, there were a few uncomfortable moments when having their father around would have helped immensely, like the time I had to answer my pubescent son's questions about some startling new hair growth. But for the most part, the kids were happily occupied with citizenship awards, sidewalk chalk masterpieces, blanket forts, flag football championships, merit badges, lemonade stands, and bowling parties during their father's yearlong absence.

And at bedtime, in the quiet darkness, when the kids had some time to consider being sad and missing Francis, they could fall asleep to the sound of his voice. He couldn't be there to read with Hayden, Anna, or Lilly, so he sent them each a little hand-held tape recorder, headphones, books, and tiny cassette tapes he'd recorded of himself reading *Black Beauty, Amelia Bedelia, Because of Winn-Dixie, Charlotte's Web, Ramona the Pest, The Westing Game*, and volumes of *A Series of Unfortunate Events*.

This isn't so bad, I thought a few months into the deployment. I'd had bouts of loneliness, but nothing that couldn't be cured with a good cry, which usually happened Friday nights around ten while watching a gut-wrenching episode of *Intervention* and eating microwave kettle corn paired with a cheap bottle of pinot noir. I'd get it all out of my system and wake up refreshed, ready to face another week on my own.

But eventually, one by one, things began to go haywire.

The hot water heater broke. I got a double ear infection and a cold sore at the same time. Hayden was bullied at school. The computer died. I said something stupid at book club. The dog dug a trench through the back yard.

Mishaps and mistakes began to pile up like the chocolates in the candy-factory episode of *I Love Lucy*. By the eighth month of our separation, I was struggling to keep up with my everyday responsibilities. The computer, phone, and social media connecting me to Francis also connected me with a world of other messages threatening to overwhelm me. I hadn't anticipated the subtle pressures brought on by our new gadgets, nipping at me like a swarm of mosquitoes, buzzing and biting relentlessly. Rather than simplifying my life, this connectivity introduced more details to my consciousness, while social media added a new layer of competitiveness and false reality.

Before Francis's deployment, I scurried busily through my days without the distraction of kitten videos, scientific breakthroughs, political banter, pop-up ads, crowdfunding campaigns, or pictures of everyone's latest meal. I had been content to read the newspaper or wait until the six o'clock news broadcast for a summary of current events. I didn't mind that the only way to find out what a friend was up to was to actually pick up the phone and call. If I wanted to know the latest trends, I could thumb through a magazine or look at the mannequins at department stores.

Suddenly, I felt the pressure to master, monitor, and manage new concepts such as teeth whitening, digital photography, hydrogenated fats, iPods, Facebook, and text messaging while handling my already-hectic schedule. I found myself drowning in a sea of meaningless minutiae—hypoallergenic pets, microbe-resistant yoga mats, antivirus software, corn syrup solids, colon cleansing, game-system updates—without a lifeline.

The increasing challenge of the deployment had knocked me off balance. The tidal wave of details and daily demands threatened to sweep me away. I lost my grip on what really mattered and was headed for a total breakdown. My Supermom days were over.

In the wee hours before dawn, I huddled in bed under the rumpled covers, squeezing the muscles of my closed eyelids in hopes of delaying the morning grind.

Something in me had snapped. I could no longer face the daily onslaught of snooze buttons, toothpaste splatters, sassy kids, and car pools. I cringed at the thought of folding laundry, scraping burnt edges off the toast, or rubbing mascara smudges from under my eyes. I couldn't deal with Anna's latest wardrobe crisis, another missing phone charger, or figuring out where I left my cup of coffee this time.

Many mornings, I just wanted to wallow in that nonsensical dream state just before full consciousness, where I might ride in a convertible Camaro with the Muppets or have a fancy-hat picnic with Marie Osmond.

For the first time since becoming a mother I felt helpless, and I couldn't stop myself from stressing about the endless details of modern family life. Something deep inside me knew I was, quite simply, overwhelmed and might not make it through the deployment without completely falling apart.

Unlike the kids, I didn't have a tape recording to get me through the night. I knew I had to do something to keep it all together.

And so, it began.

I started carrying a yellow legal pad around, making notes during piano lessons or scout meetings, wondering if jotting things down might relieve my stress just like Hayden's spiral-bound notebook had. Ever the list-maker, I wrote to-do lists, grocery lists, wish lists, and self-improvement lists. I sketched out plans for redecorating rooms and reorganizing the garage. I scribbled puns, alliterations, and interesting turns of phrase. Eventually, I began writing observations, complete sentences, and even paragraphs.

One winter night while the kids were taking swimming lessons at the overheated indoor YMCA pool, I sat on a damp bench, inhaling chlorinated steam, sweating profusely, and scribbling on my yellow legal pad.

Six lessons later, I'd lost five pounds of water weight and managed to write three personal essays about parenting, marriage, and life in the military.

I hadn't written the essays for any particular audience but writing became my way of sorting through the overwhelming details of daily life, distilling them down to what really mattered— and more importantly—what really didn't.

Writing became my lifeline.

Before I knew it Francis was home again, and we began frantically packing up to move to our next assignment in Europe. In our new apartment on Patch Barracks at US Army Garrison Stuttgart, Germany, I came up with the idea to submit my essays to newspapers for publication.

Around that same time, a humor essay I'd written about marriage titled "Tired, Boring, Predictable? True Marital Romance Is a Gas," appeared in the Metro section of *The Washington Post*.

In the following months, I filled my yellow legal pads, started a blog, and created a weekly column I called "The Meat & Potatoes of Life." I self-syndicated the column to civilian and military newspapers across the United States and eventually landed a contract with *Stars and Stripes*, the newspaper for the US Armed Forces worldwide.

Writing became my hobby, my job, my weekly therapy. It helped me realize I was human, not Supermom, and despite the chaos of the twenty-first century, there was indeed still meaning in everyday life.

Sure, I still wake up worrying: *I forgot the answers to my online security questions. I've lost track of whether faded or dark-washed denim is in style. I still don't like kale. I should've planted the daffodil bulbs earlier to adjust for global warming.*

But now, I know what to do. With my pen and yellow legal pad, I whittle life down to what counts, and I have a good laugh at all the rest.

SEASON ONE

IN THE BEGINNING

SEASON 1 ◆ EPISODE 1

WHEN STRANGERS MARRY

Twenty-five years ago, I promised to love, honor, and cherish a man I really didn't know all that well.

Before we committed ourselves to each other until death, Francis and I were pretty much clueless. We had no idea what kind of husband or wife we might turn out to be. We were in love, and we thought nothing else mattered.

Francis grew up going to private school as the son of a neurologist in the affluent DC suburb of Chevy Chase, Maryland. At weekend cocktail parties and crew regattas, his parents chatted with their friends over canapés about politics, world events, and their children's prep schools. They drank bottled water before it was trendy and bought their food from overpriced grocery stores. They kept things like capers and pâté in their refrigerators, and they drove imported cars.

I was brought up in a town with only one high school, where we thought everyone in the world had two days off for hunting season. To the people of my western Pennsylvania town, Chevy Chase was a comedian, and it was perfectly normal to get your water from a well and your meat from the woods. Our refrigerators frequently contained bricks of Velveeta, cans of Hershey's Syrup, and in the spring, fish with the heads still on. My parents' vehicles were pre-owned and, other than one Volkswagen Beetle, none were imported.

Francis grew up believing all women could throw sophisticated dinner parties at the drop of a hat, while being charming and looking fabulous in the latest styles from Lord & Taylor or Talbots. He did not realize he had made a lifetime commitment to someone who shops at Target and whose idea of a party is opening a bag of Fritos and watching a Steelers game. My poor husband has had to redefine "woman" to include those who, like me, would prefer a hot poker in the eye to the obligatory social events of a navy officer's wife.

Similarly, I have had to adjust my definition of "man" to include those who don't own fluorescent orange hunting gear, who prefer white wine to beer, and who don't require space in the garage for a work bench. I've had to come to terms with the fact that although Francis is in the navy, he is afraid of tools, guns, and knives. He shudders at the mere thought of hooking a worm, much less eating a fish with the head still on it.

I'll admit I've felt somewhat guilty for not fulfilling Francis's expectations of what his wife might be. I've often wished I were more sophisticated, formal, and fancy.

He's had his doubts about fulfilling my expectations too, like the time I put the barbecue grill together because he couldn't understand the instructions, or the beach vacation when I snorkeled for hours alone while he sipped mojitos and read an Oprah's Book Club selection under an umbrella.

We first met on the deck of my family's summer beach cottage in the Outer Banks of North Carolina. I had just come up from the beach to help out with dinner, and my mother asked if I could shuck corn before I showered. I sat cross-legged beside a pile of corn, wearing an old swimsuit, with my wet hair beginning to dry in an unflattering shape and sand ground into my ear. Just as I was shucking the third ear of corn, my brother Tray, a navy pilot, walked up onto the deck with Francis, one of his old squadron buddies.

"Lisa, this is Francis," Tray said, prompting me to squint up at him, silhouetted against the late afternoon sun. "He was our intel guy in VAQ-139 a couple years ago out in Whidbey Island."

"Nice to meet you," I said, with one eye open and a lapful of corn husks.

On the third night of his visit, Francis made me laugh at dinner. A spark was struck. We danced to Guns N' Roses' "Knockin' on Heaven's Door," which was strangely romantic, then walked to the beach to look at the stars. He was leaving the next day, but we knew we would see each other again.

When we first met, we knew for certain neither of us was perfect, but we offered each other something we were missing in our lives. Unconditional love and approval are powerful enough to transcend unknown personality quirks, but I have often wondered, *If we had known back then what we know now, would we have eternally promised ourselves to each other before the altar of Graystone Presbyterian Church all those years ago?*

Through the years, I've discovered Francis is disciplined, dedicated, and hard working. Better yet, he is fiercely loyal, and his love for our family is deep and sincere. And he still makes me laugh.

So, other than those occasions when Francis leaves his dishes in the sink or his underwear on the floor, and I contemplate running away to Mexico to sell coconuts on the beach for the rest of my life, I have no doubt the answer to the question is an undeniable:

Yes.

SEASON 1 ◆ EPISODE 2

BAGGING THE BAGGER

The day after Francis and I returned from our Bermuda honeymoon in October 1993, we moved my belongings from my parents' house in Pennsylvania to his apartment in Alexandria, Virginia, near his naval intelligence job. The morning after our move, Francis carted me around the base to get a military ID, submit health insurance forms, and obtain a pass for my car, so I could be an official, card-carrying military spouse.

Then he went to work, leaving me alone to explore our apartment.

The kitchen cupboards contained a huge plastic barrel of pretzels, a half loaf of white bread, and an expired box of Shake 'n Bake left there by his old girlfriend. In the fridge, I found a stack of bologna, a gallon of milk, a bag of onions, and a jumbo bottle of ketchup.

I'd better go shopping, I thought. I was now a navy wife, so instead of heading to the local grocery store, I hopped in the car with my new ID and braved the tangle of highways to go back to the base for my first military commissary shopping expedition.

When I got there, I was surprised to discover the commissary didn't look like a normal supermarket with colorful signs and eye-catching displays. The cavernous building's austere interior was more like a drab warehouse—just row after row of groceries.

No colorful advertising displays, no soothing background music, no free samples. The floors were painted with confusing directional arrows, pointing toward the front or back of the store. I looked for other new military spouses. Perhaps we might help each other? But there were none to be found. The employees were all business, and all the shoppers seemed to know exactly what they were doing.

I wandered aimlessly, following the big black arrows. Although my new military ID card gained me entrance into this bastion of military life, I didn't seem to belong there. I felt like a fraud, like a nineteen-year-old who just got into a nightclub with a fake ID.

I completely forgot what I needed to buy. I haphazardly threw some grapefruit, oyster crackers, a pound of ground beef, a gallon of cooking oil, and a box of raisins into my cart. I despise raisins and had never purchased oyster crackers before. Overwhelmed and unable to focus, I headed for the checkout.

The cashier looked as if she'd worked there for centuries. Her movements were automatic, and her eyes seemed fixed on some distant point. I placed my meager merchandise on the rapidly-moving conveyor belt, and the items zipped away from me. The unsmiling cashier finished scanning in a flash. Fumbling to get money out of my purse, I quipped, "Whew! You're too quick for me!" The cashier stared blankly.

A tall, thin man with a graying beard placed my paltry purchases into three plastic bags.

"Ma'am, I'll carry these to your car," he said.

"Oh no!" I said, trying to be polite, "I'll carry them myself." As I grabbed the bags and started toward the door, the smile drained from the bagger's face.

"That's your prerogative," he said, crossing his arms and turning away.

Unsure what I'd done to irritate him, I scurried back to my

car like a cockroach running under the pantry door.

Francis returned from work that evening, eager to experience his first home-cooked meal as a married man and to find out how his new wife had managed on her first day as an official military spouse.

He may have been puzzled by a dinner of meatloaf with a side dish of grapefruit, but all he said was, "So how was your day, Honey?" I related my commissary experience, and he immediately realized my mistake. He took a few minutes over dinner to explain that in military commissaries, the people who bag the groceries are not paid employees of the commissary. They work for tips. From customers. No tip means no pay.

No wonder the guy was irritated.

I had a lot to learn about being a navy wife. Rather than become overwhelmed overnight with paperwork, acronyms, customs, procedures, and unspoken rules of my new lifestyle, I decided I had plenty of time—an entire marriage, in fact—to become a seasoned military spouse. If I had to, I would bumble my way through, day by day, base by base, mistake by mistake, until I figured it out.

With my first commissary experience behind me, I adopted two new policies: Always tip the baggers, and never serve meatloaf with a side of grapefruit.

SEASON 1 ◆ EPISODE 3

DOES THIS BABY MAKE MY HUSBAND'S BUTT LOOK BIG?

"Do you want a boy or girl?" I asked, lazing in bed, seven months pregnant on a Saturday morning in 1995. Francis and I gazed languidly through the lace sheers billowing over our bedroom window at the sun-soaked cypress tree in our little Fort Ord, California, back yard.

Without the early morning responsibilities a baby would soon bring to our weekends, we were free to lie around, listen to the chirping birds, and wonder what our life might bring.

On sunny weekends, we might hike in Big Sur, stop at a local restaurant for fresh Monterey Bay squid steaks, or visit our friends' house near Lovers Point for cookouts. On rainy Saturdays and Sundays, we rolled from our bed to the living room couch, watching old movies late into the afternoon in sweatpants and slippers, only running out for popcorn and take out.

We believed working all week entitled us to self-indulgent weekends. Little did we know—after less than two years of marriage—having a baby would strip us of that luxury for good.

"Well," Francis responded after a pause to imagine our future as parents, "I think I'd look good carrying a girl around."

How odd, I thought.

I had assumed my question would prompt him to compare and contrast the experiences he might have raising a son or daughter. Would he want to fish with his son? Throw baseballs in the yard? Or would he prefer to be called into his daughter's room for tea parties? Instead, Francis expressed his preference for a boy or a girl based solely upon which one might complement *his physical appearance.*

"What do you mean, *you'd look good* carrying a girl around?" I hoped this man with his arm draped possessively over my swollen belly was not a closet narcissist intent on using his offspring as a wardrobe accessory.

"You know what I mean," he retorted, clearly assuming anyone when asked the same question would think first of his appearance. "When I imagine being a father, I see myself walking around with a little girl wearing pink booties and a lace bonnet and all that." He went on to describe how other people might see him in public and think, "Oh, look how cute that dad is over there, carrying his sweet little baby girl."

I listened, trying desperately to understand Francis's point of view, but I was worried. *Are we too selfish to be parents?*

"It's a boy!" the obstetrician announced two months later. Hayden Clark Molinari entered our world on a rainy spring evening in 1995 weighing in at nine pounds. Selfish or not, ready or not, Francis and I became parents.

In an instant, our priorities were forever reordered. We lost ourselves in a blur of diapers, bottles, blankets, booties, thermometers, teensy nail clippers, and early morning feedings. Francis didn't notice I looked like I'd been hit by a Mack truck, and I couldn't have cared less he was wearing the same spit-up-stained sweatshirt for three days in a row. We were too caught up in the sheer wonder of the little bundle of ten toes and ten fingers we'd created.

The rest of the world simply melted away.

Francis eventually got his baby girls. Anna—who came out with an inordinate number of dimples in her chin, cheeks, knees, knuckles, and tush—was born under the stern but gentle direction of an Irish midwife while we were stationed in Molesworth, England, in 1998. Anna would become our talker, driven to create and implement her own ideas, which usually involved bossing her little sister around.

Lilly came during our next tour in Virginia and was the quintessential third child: happy-go-lucky, resigned to being bossed around by her older siblings, and content to tag along.

Although Francis no longer mused about how his children made him look, he never completely gave up his interest in his own appearance. Parenthood didn't cure him of checking himself out in shop windows, even sneaking a peek at his backside, or demanding to be photographed when feeling particularly dapper. On the dance floor, he still played to the crowd, forgetting he was supposed to be dancing with me.

But, when we became parents, Francis's responsibility to our family became his main concern. To me, there's nothing more attractive.

SEASON 1 ◆ EPISODE 4

PORK CHOP ENVY

It was another gloomy winter afternoon in our working-class English village. While we were stationed in the sleepy village of Molesworth in the flat Cambridgeshire countryside, I often found myself counting the minutes until Francis got home from work.

At that latitude, the sun set around four o'clock, leaving me with nothing to do but pop in a Barney video for Hayden and contemplate dinner.

One day, I wandered nonchalantly to the pantry to examine the usual lineup of canned vegetables, dried noodles, and jarred pickles. And there it was—staring at me from between the peanut butter and salsa with smug indignation—a box of Shake 'n Bake. It had belonged to the woman who had come before me in Francis's life. She had bought it, presumably, for a cozy dinner with the man who was now my husband.

Melissa was Francis's old girlfriend. Somehow, her Shake 'n Bake, along with her gawd-awful dining room chairs and etched wine glasses, had become mingled with our joint marital property when Francis and I got married. Somehow, even after three more moves, the Shake 'n Bake had survived.

I accepted the chairs and glasses out of necessity—we needed all the hand-me-downs we could get in those days—but what were we still doing with this lousy box of Shake 'n Bake?

I don't use tawdry cooking shortcuts, I thought. It was cheap, just like Melissa with her frizzy red hair, overdone makeup, and Boy George hats. I wanted to be rid of this relic of Francis's past life, once and for all. The vacuum-sealed pouch of pork chop coating might have expired, but I sentenced it to death. I grabbed the offending box from the shelf and headed for the rubbish bin.

But wait, I thought. *Why not use this as a teaching moment?*

The mixture seemed surprisingly fresh for its age, more than four years old. I followed the package instructions, throwing meat into the bag with the pouch ingredients and laying the coated pieces out on a cookie sheet.

When Francis arrived home, the "Melissa Memorial Dinner" was ready.

While Francis changed out of his uniform, I eagerly anticipated his reaction to the meal. I envisioned the disappointment that would most certainly appear on his face as he bit into the cheapened chop. I would ask innocently, "Do you like it, Honey? I made it with that old box of crumb coating. Wasn't it—oh, what's her name again—Melissa? Wasn't it Melissa's Shake 'n Bake?"

Surely, he would spit the bite into his napkin and declare the meal a culinary embarrassment. He would confess I was a much better cook than Melissa. He would realize again why I was the love of his life and Melissa was a mistake.

"Smells good," Francis said as I doled pork, green beans, and potatoes onto his plate. He carved a particularly large bite of meat, plunged it into his potatoes and opened wide.

I watched intently for a grimace, a groan, a gag.

"Mmhmm," Francis mumbled, shoveling forkfuls into his mouth. I waited patiently for my opportunity to blame Melissa for his inevitable disgust.

"This is delicious, Hon," Francis said, spearing a second chop. I nibbled a bite myself and had to concede he was right. The Shake 'n Bake wasn't half bad after all.

My insecurities had driven me to kill an innocent box of bread crumbs, trying to burn an old girlfriend in effigy. But the Shake 'n Bake wasn't a threat to my marriage any more than she was.

I sheepishly confessed my plot, and we both laughed hard at my ridiculousness. I raised a glass to Melissa, giving credit where credit was due, and promised to make her signature recipe again.

After all, it wasn't a mistake; it was just Shake 'n Bake.

SEASON 1 ◆ EPISODE 5

SILENCE ISN'T GOLDEN, IT'S GREEN

When our children were small, I'd yell into our playroom on a regular basis: "Kids…what's going on in there?!"

Usually, I heard roughhousing, giggling, knocks against the wall, creaking couch springs, yips, and squeals. You'd think the innocent sounds of our children playing would warm our hearts, but Francis and I knew those wholesome noises often led to bonked heads, chipped teeth, and poked eyes.

Other times, we heard no squeals, bumps, or creaking floorboards. No singing, hammering, smacking, or crying. No Barbies being thrown, sippy cups hitting the floor, or lamps getting knocked over.

What we heard was something far more terrifying: total silence.

At the best of times, kids are noisy. They sniffle, babble, fidget, fiddle, and whine. Silence is a clear sign something's wrong.

Case in point: One night, when our family was stationed in Virginia, before Lilly came along, Francis and I let our five-year-old son, Hayden, and his two-year-old sister, Anna, watch a video in the playroom before bedtime.

Back in those days, we savored every peaceful second a half-hour video provided, as if it were some kind of luxurious spa treatment. As soon as we popped a tape into the VCR, we dashed down the stairs to melt into our couch cushions. With the doors open, we could hear the murmur of the often-played video and the sounds of our kids tinkering with toys. After countless nights of the same routine, we knew exactly when our babysitter time was up.

But on that night, the half hour flew by without us noticing. Twenty minutes or so after *Arthur* was over, I nudged Francis. "Uh oh...I don't hear the kids."

"Hayden and Anna!" Francis yelled up the playroom stairs, "What's going on in there?"

Soon we heard little padded feet scurrying and intermittent giggling. Hayden and Anna slunk downstairs and appeared before us with their heads bowed in guilt. When they looked up, we saw they each had green marker scribbled all over their hands and faces.

"What have you two been doing?" we demanded. Anna's enormous brown eyes flashed to her older brother.

"Playing," Hayden said.

"Hayden and Anna, you're not supposed to use markers on skin," I scolded. Reaching for a tub of baby wipes, I noticed green marks on Anna's neck dipping below the collar of her footed pajamas. I unzipped her pjs and gasped.

Anna's chest, belly, arms, legs, feet, hands, and back were a green, inky mess. A quick inspection of Hayden revealed pristine skin. Other than his green hands and face, he was marker-free. The culprit was obvious.

"Hayden! Why did you scribble all over your little sister?" Francis pressed.

"Not me," Hayden shrugged.

"Then how did *your* name get in the middle of Anna's back? Do you expect us to believe she put it there? She can't even write her name yet!" I barked.

We looked down at our sheepish kids, realizing Hayden had

pulled off a classic big brother prank on his adoring little sister. Francis and I tried to maintain a serious demeanor, but one side glance at each other was all it took to get us laughing.

Pretty soon, all four of us were cracking up. Anna had no idea what was so funny, but she laughed right along with us.

After a second round of baths to remove the washable marker, we tucked them into bed for the night. We stopped by the playroom to turn out the lights, still smiling about their sweet shenanigans.

The grins drained from our faces when we saw what the kids had really been up to. The tattooing of Anna had been only practice doodles. The real masterpiece was on the formerly pale-yellow walls of the playroom. Somehow, in the time it took for us to realize the *Arthur* video had ended, Hayden had managed to create a mural of scribbles on all four walls in every color of the rainbow.

And he did it in complete silence.

Whoever said "children should be seen, not heard" clearly wasn't a parent.

SEASON 1 ◆ EPISODE 6

RULE NO. 1: FOLLOW THE RULES

I always wanted to be one of those moms who could handle anything, and for the most part I was. I cooked, I cleaned, I nurtured, I maintained complete control. Nothing could faze me.

It worked for a while, until, strangely, my children started to think for themselves. No amount of time-outs, gold stars, groundings, or "wait-till-your-father-gets-homes" would convince my children to obey me every time.

My breaking point came during a family camping trip near Yorktown, Virginia. Ever the idealist, I envisioned hilarious family game nights in the cabin, meaningful talks on the docks under dappled sunlight, delicious barbecues, and gooey fireside s'mores.

It rained for four days solid.

Thankfully, our cabin was equipped with electricity, and the sedative effect of the television was the only thing keeping us from going mad. On the fifth day, the clouds parted, and I was determined to salvage the experience with a perfect family barbecue.

We cooked hotdogs over a few sad charcoal briquettes, while the kids ran amok, squealing and fighting, around the muddy perimeter of our camp.

I set the algae-stained picnic table with paper plates and

channeled June Cleaver, "C'mon kiddos! Time for din-din!"

When no one showed, I started to count, "One, two..."

Only Lilly appeared, splattered with mud to her knees, so I stormed off to physically escort Hayden and Anna to their seats.

"I don't wanna eat it," Anna said, staring down at her cold mac-n-cheese and singed hot dog.

"No shoe," Lilly mumbled, just as I noticed her purple mary jane embedded in the mud a few feet away. I swatted the gnats and tried to maintain my composure.

I was sure s'mores would be a hit. We held the marshmallows against the metal grill to find heat from the smoldering briquettes. But in the end, the sugary confections were stiff and tainted with black soot and hot dog residue. The kids were too busy fighting over Hershey bars to notice.

Finally, we gave up. The cabin's electronic nanny—the television—lulled the kids into a catatonic state, and Francis and I collapsed onto the couch. Frustrated with my lack of control, my mind raced.

Just then, the proverbial light bulb blinked on in my head. I leaped off the couch to find the art supplies I had packed for happy family crafts we never did and scribbled like a mad scientist working out an ingenious formula. An hour later, my masterpiece was complete: The Molinari Family Rules were born.

At home a few days later, I was determined to set a new and improved standard for our family.

"Ahem. I hereby call to order the first official Molinari Family Meeting. Please take a moment to write your name at the top of the four-page agenda I typed up this morning," I proclaimed while pushing in Lilly's booster seat.

I unveiled The Rules in dramatic fashion and asked everyone to read them aloud with me and discuss each rule in detail. After fifteen minutes, the kids slouched in their seats. After half an hour, their heads drooped onto the table. By the forty-five-minute mark, Francis was nodding off, so I ended on a positive note something about how much I loved them—and hoped my message had sunk in.

Several such meetings have taken place since that ill-fated camping trip. Every time I feel things spinning out of control, I call another meeting. I always ask everyone to recite The Rules together. After each meeting, I feel rejuvenated, armed, and in control again.

But at some point, it dawned on me: no one's behavior really changed much after our family meetings. Perhaps the meetings were only for my benefit.

Maybe everyone in the family put up with family meetings just for me, so I could regain my sanity.

Oh, well, at the very least, it meant they had mastered Rule No. 1: "Be kind."

SEASON 1 ◆ EPISODE 7

HOW YOU PLAY THE GAME

When Hayden was a squishy little ten-year-old, he preferred piano and rainbows to athletic pursuits. However, early in the fall of his fifth-grade year, Hayden started showing an interest in football. As visions of tailgate parties danced in our heads, we jumped on the opportunity and contacted the local flag football league.

"Sorry ma'am, the teams are full. Now if your husband would be willing to coach, your son could play this season."

Completely ignorant of the league team selection process, Francis agreed.

We received a roster of fifteen kids—Hayden and fourteen others who transferred from overcrowded teams. We soon realized that each of the coaches had been asked to give up a couple of kids, and of course they picked their worst players.

Oblivious, we showed up for our first practice raring and ready to access the boys' talents. The lineup was not what we expected.

None of the boys knew a thing about football. But they were all excited to play. We named the team the Sharks and accepted the rejected purple league jerseys without complaint. Practice looked more like children who were running from a fire than executing planned plays, but we were hopeful it would all come together on game day.

With Francis as the coach, I became the team mom, and I admit I went overboard. I bought the soundtrack from *Jaws*. I bought sweatshirts, t-shirts, and purple towels. I made up cheers.

Game day finally arrived, and we were ready. Parents donned their Sharks spirit wear and swung their little purple towels. Players gathered around Coach Francis for a pregame pep talk.

"Listen boys, I want you all to go out there today and show 'em what you're made of! Let's tell everybody, if you swim with the Sharks, you're gonna get bit!"

Both players and parents alike exploded into simultaneous applause and collective woo-hoos.

A half hour later, we were down by three touchdowns, and our blissful ignorance of the league team selection process ended abruptly.

"Listen up, Sharks!" Francis barked during half time, "Don't let the numbers on that scoreboard get you down! We are the Sharks! Win or lose, we are gonna fight and fight hard! Now go out there, boys, and give 'em all you got!"

At the end of the third quarter, the ref called the game because they were beating us forty to zilch.

The rest of the season was more of the same, and it was not easy to keep the morale of our little Sharks above water. Instead of emphasizing winning, we became determined to surprise the other team with our undying spirit.

We waved our purple towels, blared the *Jaws* theme song, and shouted our original Sharks cheers. No matter the odds against us, the Sharks played every game to win.

We never scored one point.

The following year, I ran into a former Sharks mom at a local grocery store. She said even though her son was placed on a winning team that fall, he confessed, "Mom, I wish this team was more like the Sharks."

In spite of losing every game, the Sharks were a winning team after all.

SEASON 1 ◆ EPISODE 8

CHEESEBALLS, PERVERTS, AND OTHER FINANCIAL ADVISORS

Nothing spells financial panic like looking into the eyes of your newborn baby.

Before Hayden was born, Francis and I dreamed our savings would go toward Caribbean getaways and self-indulgent automobile purchases. We had no idea the "fun" in our "fun money" would be sucked dry like formula from a bottle, and we would eventually be scrambling to save money just to give the little tyke a fighting chance in the world.

Soon after Hayden was born, we called for help.

We used a financial planning company that specialized in advising military families. Once enrolled in the company's program, we were connected with a financial advisor who was assigned to the US military base near our home in England.

When our new financial advisor arrived at our door, we thought he was going to tell us exactly what we needed to do to avoid certain disaster. But he had other plans. He sat with us at our economical Montgomery Ward kitchen table and rattled off a canned series of rhetorical questions from a script in his faux-leather three-ring binder.

"Do you want financial security for your family?"

"Would it make you proud to send your kids to college?"

"Would you like to retire with enough to pay your bills?"

As he posed the absurd, rehearsed questions, Francis and I glanced sideways at each other. We knew with each cautious "yes," we were leading him through a flow chart ending with us forking over a bunch of money, so this guy could earn a commission. Although we were both disappointed our would-be financial savior turned out to be a cheesy salesman, we couldn't help but see the humor in the situation.

After the painful presentation, we politely led the financial planner out and waved toodle-oo. As soon as the door clicked shut, Francis and I doubled over with pent-up laughter. We spent the rest of the night asking each other ridiculous rhetorical questions.

"Is it your dream to have edible food for tonight's dinner?"

"Do you enjoy the feeling of good dental hygiene after brushing?"

"Is it your ambition to have hot coffee in the morning?"

When we moved to our new duty station in Virginia, we set up an appointment to meet another advisor. Arriving at his office, we were relieved by his straightforward style. After very little small talk, he got right to it. No canned series of questions, no faux-leather three-ring binders, no glossy pie charts with pretty colors.

This short, bald man knew his stuff, and we knew he was there to help us. He scrambled excitedly around his office like a chipmunk, gathering our financial nuts and building our little nest egg for the future.

At one point in the meeting, he was having some difficulty getting us to understand the various options for setting up college funds. He tried simple verbal descriptions, dry erase board drawings, and even hand motions. Seeing us still dazed, he scurried behind his desk to retrieve an explanatory graph he had saved on his computer.

As he plopped his plump frame into his oversized leather

chair, he swung the monitor around so we could see it. At that moment, the screensaver photo of his wife and kids blinked off, and we could hardly believe our eyes. In its place was a full-screen photo of a woman posing seductively in skimpy lingerie, advertising a local "After-Dark Escort Service." Our sense of relief over finding a trustworthy consultant was shattered.

After a split second of intense shock, our little financial guru swung the monitor out of our view, found the college fund chart file, and began nervously jabbering away about 529 plans as if we had not seen his dark secret.

We said our goodbyes and headed for the parking lot.

Although we got a good laugh out of the situation, we wondered if there were any decent, honest people out there who could give us good advice about our personal finances. Third time's the charm, they say, but we were skeptical about finding Mr. Right.

Waiting in the lobby of our third financial guy's office, we speculated he might be in the witness protection program or on parole for a double murder.

A receptionist brought us Styrofoam cups of coffee and led us to an office filled with family photos, basketball trophies, and children's artwork. As we waited, we wondered if the poor family in the photos knew their husband/father was really a hit man for the mob.

After a few minutes, our new financial manager walked into the room with a folder under one arm and a World's Greatest Dad coffee cup in the other. He was tall, wore glasses, and had a warm smile. We imagined the horror the tellers must've experienced when he robbed all those banks at gunpoint.

He introduced himself as Stanley, and we began to talk.

By our fourth or fifth meeting, Stanley was so exasperated with our suspicions, he slumped into his chair, put his hands over his eyes and said, "Do you have *any* idea how little money I make from your account?" Dropping his hands onto his lap, he said, "Exactly eleven dollars and seventy-five cents a month."

Slowly but surely, Stanley won our trust. He and his family lived nearby, and we ran into them at school functions and community events. He chatted with Francis and me at a Cub Scout meeting one night, wearing a large dried-up splotch of spaghetti sauce on his chin. To us, the spaghetti sauce represented Stanley's private life and revealed, perhaps, he had nothing to hide.

We contact Stanley every year, and he helps us manage our money. He may not be Charles Schwab, Merrill Lynch, or T. Rowe Price.

But we're just happy he's not an axe murderer.

SEASON 1 ◆ EPISODE 9

AIRING DIRTY LAUNDRY

Each summer our extended family of eleven squeezed into a 1970s beach cottage that slept ten uncomfortably. Like one of those bad reality shows, our annual vacation on the Outer Banks of North Carolina began with a chaotic dash for the good beds. Suitcases exploded, turning the previously tidy old cottage into a veritable landfill. Floors became littered with swimsuits, towels, and toys; countertops with soda cans, chips, sunglasses, lotion, shells, coffee cake, peanuts, and sticky spots from spilled daiquiri mix.

The cast of our reality show included me, Francis, and our three kids; my mother, Diane, affectionately called Maz the Spaz; my brother Tray, his Canadian wife, Jacqueline, and their three children. Tray and Jacq raised a fit family of type-A personalities who aggressively and successfully fought for whatever life had to offer. Francis and I, both a bit soft and squishy literally and figuratively, raised our kids to be B-plus personalities, who appreciated eccentricities and a reasonable level of mediocrity.

Our combined six kids brought goofy exuberance, infuriating sass, angsty brooding, attention-seeking, and plenty of whining to the table.

Adding to family tension among the cast, my cantankerous father Durwood and his second wife Sherri retired to a house a few blocks away from the cottage, and a myriad of other odd relatives would drop in to visit while we were there. Consequently, the drama of our annual vacation was more akin to *The Perfect Storm* than *Beach Blanket Bingo*.

Even though the size of the beach cottage we occupied necessitated us being physically close, we all tried to avoid learning intimate details about each other during our shared vacation time. For the first few days we maintained a façade of virtue, cleanliness, and self-control. However, after two weeks, awkward personal secrets were inevitably revealed, the crude realities of life exposed.

Toiletry bags in the shared bathrooms divulged our need for embarrassing pharmaceuticals, such as stool softeners and anti-fungal ointments. Meals together revealed whether we put too much mayonnaise on our sandwiches, dipped into the chips every couple of hours, or got caught taking another brownie from the pan. When we dozed off on the couch, everyone saw the unflattering ways our mouths fell open and chins multiplied when we slept. And commingled laundry allowed everyone to bear witness to the sometimes-alarming size of some of our undergarments.

"Whose are these?" Jacq said one day, laughing and holding up a large pair of underwear from a basket of warm laundry. Voices rang out from around our beach cottage.

"Whoa! Not mine!" came from the couch.

"Me neither!" broadcasted from the staircase.

"Mine aren't THAT big!" emanated from the hallway.

"Uh, yeah," I admitted sheepishly, "those would be mine, thank you very much."

I claimed my stack of folded clothes and slunk off to my room.

This kind of humiliation was just part of the family vacation experience. Whoever volunteered to fold clothes would become privy to the size of everyone else's underwear, setting up perfect opportunities to crack jokes. Admittedly, my Jockeys "For Her" were ample enough to fold over several times, while my thinner relatives' teensy-weensy skivvies were constructed with so little material, I once mistook a pair of my niece's underwear for a hair scrunchie.

When vacationing with my relatives, harassment, brow-beating, rude sarcasm, and relentless needling fell under the category of playful banter. My family considered these personal pot shots a kind of vacation-time sporting event, like cornhole or ladder ball.

Over the course of my summer beach vacations—when one of my relatives said the mole on my chin looked like it was growing an eye or offered to put Metamucil in my daiquiri to help out with my "little problem," or imitated my dance moves to make the cousins laugh—I learned the best plan was to let it go and laugh along.

And, most importantly, always fold my own laundry.

SEASON 1 ◆ EPISODE 10

TRUE LOVE IS A GAS

One busy night after the kids had gone to bed, I settled into my well-worn spot on the sofa for some mind-numbing television.

"Can you believe this guy?" I asked Francis, gesturing at whoever was blathering away on TV. Francis, seated in his favorite recliner beside me, didn't answer. I glanced over to witness an all-too-familiar scene: Deeply embedded in the recliner's cushions, my husband slept soundly.

Normally, I would giggle, turn the lights out around him and go to bed—a sort of revenge for being "abandoned" for the umpteenth time. Francis would eventually wake up alone in the dark and trudge upstairs to find me tee-heeing under the covers of our bed.

But on this particular night, I gawked at my dreaming husband as if I were seeing this for the first time. Is this the man I married?

Panic gripped my soul as I realized: We're tired, boring, predictable. *We're doomed.*

I remember one evening in 1992, my fiancé, Francis, and I were at an Italian café in Pittsburgh, sipping wine and falling in love.

"I really want to travel," I said. "Me too," he said. "I want to live near the ocean," he said. "Me too," I said. "I don't care about money, I just want happiness," he said. "Me too!" I said. It was a match made in heaven and our future was destined to be perfect.

But maybe if we had understood the reality of marriage our conversation would have been different.

Me: "I might have a lot of stretch marks."

Him: "That's okay, we'll just dim the lights."

Him: "I'm going to go bald, but ironically, hair will sprout out of my ears and nose."

Me: "I'm good with tweezers."

Him: "I have no mechanical ability whatsoever and will feel no embarrassment if my wife handles all the home repairs."

Me: "I won't have a problem with that for the first ten years or so, but then I'll get fed up."

But back then, we weren't thinking about annoying habits, taxes, and clogged drains. We were too busy planning our perfect life.

Our unrealistic expectations persisted after we were engaged. "Oh, pardon me!" Francis yelped after accidentally belching. Although he insisted he would *never* expel any kind of gas in front of me, it didn't take long for his steely resolve to erode. Expelling gas is commonplace. It happens mid-sentence, under the covers, in the recliner.

Before marriage, I preened and pampered Francis like a primate, manicuring nails and plucking stray hairs to maintain his ruggedly handsome good looks. I thought this giddy nurturing stage would last forever; I had no idea those stray hairs would later multiply so profusely that our grooming sessions would eventually take place in the garage and involve the leaf blower. The pedicures became completely intolerable after my husband's left piggy toe grew to resemble a tiny hoof. One of the kids asked him if it was made out of wood.

I had to draw the line somewhere.

Are we doomed because we haven't met our premarital

expectations?

That night as I watched Francis dozing, I realized something very important: We did not *meet* our original expectations, we *exceeded* them. Back when we were dreaming of a life of romance uninhibited by responsibility, stress, and aging, we couldn't fully comprehend the complexity and depth of the marital relationship.

We didn't understand that romance is more than candlelight dinners and adventurous travel. The foundation of long-term romance is commitment, companionship, and comfort.

My initial annoyance at the sight of my sleeping husband turned to a sort of sweet adoration. As I turned the lights out and sneaked upstairs to wait for him to wake up alone in the dark, I felt happy our marriage turned out to be better than I'd ever imagined.

SEASON TWO

IN THE MIX

SEASON 2 ◆ EPISODE 1

TOTALLY TUBULAR

The summer we moved to Germany, I stood by without uttering a word of protest as I watched Anna and Lilly race downhill in our new neighborhood riding in an abandoned shopping cart. Anna gripped the handle and gave the cart a big push. Balancing her hips on the handle, she lifted both feet off the ground and leaned into the wind. Lilly sat in the basket holding on for dear life. Both girls were clearly loving every second, each in her own way.

Call it counterintuitive for a mother to allow her daughters to engage in potentially unsafe play. Call it negligent parenting if you like. I call it nostalgia. I grew up with an older brother, so although I wasn't present for the pre-ride planning, I knew exactly how this event transpired. Clearly, the shopping cart ride was Anna's doing.

Anna was a born instigator. As an infant, supported by parental hands, she would stiffen her legs and stand up as though insisting on independence. At six months, she pointed a slobbery finger at Zuzu, our fat runt of a cat, and slurred, "kitty-kitty-kitty." Francis and I knew Anna was clever, but we did not understand her precociousness indicated a rapidly-developing need to be in control.

By age three, she had an opinion about everything. She loved making friends as long as she could be the one making all the decisions. Throughout childhood, Anna's best friends were those who were content to let her be the boss. She practiced dominance and manipulation regularly on everyone, particularly her little sister, Lilly.

Lilly was an easy-going baby. No doubt her low-key temperament was partly the result of her birth order. She didn't fuss or cry for attention while I attended to her needy older siblings. While I worked in the kitchen, she entertained herself, playing with pots and pans, or splashing in a makeshift bath in the sink. I carried her in the Snugli or on my hip while I multitasked, cutting up onions, blowing leaves, or opening cereal boxes. She was content to tag along during errands, in and out of car seats, therapists' waiting rooms, and shopping carts.

From the start, Lilly idolized her big sister and happily accepted her role as Anna's protégé. She clearly had her own personality and sense of humor but never showed any desire to be the center of attention. Through many military moves, Lilly had a gift for finding herself a best friend on the first day at a new school and maintaining these relationships long term. People were attracted to Lilly by her sensitivity to others' feelings and her desire to make them happy. If Lilly was around when Francis and I were having an argument, she might walk into the room and say something like, "Wow, you look really handsome today, Daddy."

Lilly's innate qualities made her the perfect foil for Anna, the faithful, willing companion for whatever Anna dreamed up. When we moved to Germany, Anna adopted the phrase, "Adventure awaits!" At the airport, at home, at the dog park, in the neighborhood playground, in the commissary, Anna would goad Lilly into hair-brained but creative schemes.

Having had a dominant older brother whom I once idolized, I completely understood why Lilly agreed to go along with Anna's plans, including the shopping cart ride.

One summer back in the seventies, my brother Tray and his friend Tracy scored two large inner tubes. Tray and Tracy were in junior high school, way too cool for little sisters like me. So I trotted barefoot up the hill to the neighbor's backyard playhouse, picking newly-sprouted dandelions along the way.

About an hour later, there was a knock at the playhouse door.

"Hey, Lisa! C'mere! Wanna do something fun with me and Tracy?!"

Flabbergasted by this unusual turn of events, I threw the baby doll I had been tenderly rocking into the spider-webbed corner and ran out the door.

"Whaddya wanna do?!" I yelled excitedly.

Tray and Tracy led me to the side of the neighbors' house where I saw the inner tubes lashed together, side by side, with twine. Grinning sideways at his friend and down at me, my brother said, "Lisa, if you climb inside the tubes, we'll roll you down the hill and it'll be really fun!"

I didn't see red flags or hear alarm bells. All I knew was my big brother finally wanted to play with me.

I crouched down and climbed into the center hole, gripping the metal valves like handles just as they instructed. With my chin on my chest and my legs crisscrossed, I fit snuggly into the tiny space. Assuring me the ride would be better than the Scrambler at the county fair, they carefully shoved me off down the hill.

As the tubes took their first few rotations, I squealed with excitement. But when I reached the drop off at the front of the neighbors' property, the cylinder spun wildly with the sudden acceleration. The natural undulations of the lawn sent the tubes airborne, causing them to change shape as they bounced on the ground. The circle distorted into an elongated oval, and with each impact my teeth clacked.

As the contraption flew down the hill toward a border of blue spruces, my initial squeals of delight turned into screams of terror and then into the silence of survival mode. From my cramped vantage point, I could see flashes of blue sky, the approaching spruces, grass, and Tray and Tracy screaming down the hill after me.

I knew I had to save myself from certain disaster. As I slammed into the ground after a particularly high bounce, I stuck my foot out of the ring. My toes immediately caught the grass, flipping the tubes like a quarter in a coin toss.

My wheel of terror teetered to a stop just before the spruces, and I burst out of the confining hole onto the grass. The entire universe spun around me. I could hear faint yelling growing louder as Tracy got closer, until his silhouette appeared against the blue sky above me.

"Lisa! Lisa! Are you okay?!" Tracy panted, as a drop of spit began to ooze from his gaping mouth. Just before the elongating globule could detach itself, he slurped and swallowed in the nick of time.

As the summers passed, my brother continued to bait me into painful judo flips, terrifying locked closets, and other ill-judged schemes, and I also found plenty of trouble all on my own. In an ironically comforting way, seeing Anna and Lilly speeding downhill in the shopping cart confirmed for me the natural order of the world. Children will always seek adventure, often dragging along their unsuspecting siblings. Some things in life never change.

SEASON 2 ◆ EPISODE 2

MUSIC TO MY EARS

I ran through the doors of the elementary school and breathlessly scribbled my name on the sign-in sheet.

"Would you please tell me where the music room is?" I asked, somewhat embarrassed not to know. Lilly had been a student there for two years while our family was stationed in Stuttgart, Germany, but this was my first visit to the music room. In fact, I had barely set foot in the school all year, but Lilly begged me to *please* show up for this event, the recorder recital for her music class.

"Down the hall to the end, make a right, second door on your left," the secretary answered without looking up from her computer.

Mindful of school rules about running in the halls, I scurried to the music room, hoping the fourth-grade recital had not yet begun, even though I was ten minutes late.

As the third child, Lilly definitely got the short end of the stick, as our interest in school events waned over the years. The week before, I had forgotten to pick up Lilly from school. And it was raining. When I realized my error, I rushed out of our apartment, jumped into the minivan, and gunned it up the hill toward the school. Just then I saw her, happily running alone down the sidewalk, arms outstretched and eyes closed, her backpack flopping under the bob of her sandy brown hair. As fat raindrops splatted on her sweet face, she grinned from ear to ear with pure joy.

That was Lilly. She deserved so much more than we gave her. I knew I had to be at her recorder recital.

Wearing my workout clothes, a muddy pair of running shoes, and a visor to cover my bed head, I hoped the recital would be over quickly, so I could get to the base commissary to do some grocery shopping before the lunchtime rush.

I found the music room and gingerly turned the doorknob until it clicked. As I pushed it open, I could see everyone in the room looking back at me—parents crammed against the wall in folding chairs and students standing on two rows of risers.

Lilly was on the top row. Her eyes widened when she saw me at the door, and she bit her bottom lip to control a grin.

"COME IN!" the music teacher bellowed from her seat behind the keyboard. Startled, I scuttled into the room and took the first seat I could find, as the teacher continued her program.

"Again! From the top! Stand up straight! Hands at your sides!" she yelled at the group of twenty boys and girls from Ms. Farnsworth's fourth grade class. She pounded out the notes on the keyboard, and the kids started singing at her head-bobbed cue.

"Be the best, best, best you can be, be, be!" they wailed, some with deadpan stiffness, and others with dramatic inflection. The song entailed a complicated Bingo-like start-stop game in succeeding verses and a few of the kids flubbed and shouted out "best" or "be" when they were supposed to be silent.

At the end of the song, the teacher's deep voice boomed from behind the keyboard, "I give you a two-point-five out of four! The only thing I accept in this classroom is a four! Backs straight! AGAIN, from the top!" I jerked out of my slouch and sat up obediently, afraid to move. I was taken aback by this teacher's demanding treatment, and I tried to see in my peripheral vision if the other parents looked as concerned as I felt. But they all sat straight-backed at attention, as though afraid to look at each other.

As the kids made their next attempt, I was mystified by their cheerful obedience to this drill-sergeant of a music teacher. They belted the tune out in perfect order this time, each of them with their eyes locked on their leader, only occasionally glancing at a parent out of sheer personal pride.

"Now THAT'S a four! Like I always tell you boys and girls, you don't have to BE the best, but you must DO your best every time!" The children beamed and looked to their parents for appreciation.

"COME IN!" the teacher repeated, and I noticed a father in uniform sneaking in the back and taking a seat. He exchanged blown kisses with his daughter, who radiated joy over seeing him there.

"Parents and students, sing the chorus!" The music teacher proceeded to lead us all in a peppy rendition of "You're a Grand Old Flag," complete with choreographed hand movements. Through three repeats, she belted out verses in her sharp booming voice, with a rumbling vibrato akin to Ethel Merman, while we all fumbled to achieve perfection in the cramped music room.

"Excellent! That's the best you have done! I am so proud of you!" she roared at everyone. The kids seemed to love their teacher's brawny leadership and relentless drive and basked in her praise for their accomplishments.

The teacher ordered the kids into new positions, and each one approached her in turn to pick up their assigned recorder flute. In two neat rows they sat, gripping their little plastic instruments as they awaited her instruction.

She snapped out instructions as the kids whipped their recorders into position like a well-rehearsed drill team.

"I'm a task master, and I make no apologies for it! Now, don't hurt your parents' ears!" she roared. The irony made me giggle. The kids blew a surprisingly soothing version of "Hot Cross Buns" into the recorders with only an occasional rogue squeaky note.

Despite this teacher's sovereignty over this tight ship of a crowded classroom, I found myself being seized by tenderness and nearly tearing up. Why? I've heard "Hot Cross Buns" a million times, not exactly a sentimental ditty. I've been to so many seemingly insignificant little school events. But as I sat there watching Lilly working so hard to make me proud, I realized these moments were fleeting and precious.

Feelings of guilt over my grubby outfit and my failure to bring a camera were interrupted when the teacher jumped from her seat and yelled, "Good job! I am very proud of you! BUCKET!" At that command, the beaming students brought their instruments up one by one and dropped them neatly into a blue bucket.

"When your name is called, come up and get your certificate and pencil! Parents: CLAP!" she ordered, and I was again seized by emotion watching my sweet little girl so happy to receive a symbolic piece of paper and a ten-cent pencil with music notes painted on it.

"DISMISSED!" our leader yelled one last time. As we exited the classroom in orderly fashion, I found Lilly and gave her a long squeeze.

"Thank you for coming Mommy," she muffled into my shirt.

"I wouldn't have missed this for the world," I answered, truthfully.

SEASON 2 ◆ EPISODE 3

REVIVAL OF THE FITTEST

"I'm getting sick," Francis proclaimed one afternoon when he came in the door from work. He dropped his briefcase as if it were filled with rocks. He allowed his coat to fall off his shoulders and onto the floor and left it there as if hanging it on one of the convenient hooks right beside the door was just too much. He shuffled dramatically toward the living room couch, stopping at one point to cough so theatrically, I expected him to take a bow. Upon reaching the sofa, he glanced in my direction, presumably to see if I was watching, before disengaging all of his muscles and plopping onto the couch as if he had just lost consciousness.

"Nnngggmmmmuuuhhh," was his elongated groan before the curtain came down.

I watched this display from the kitchen without the slightest sense of compassion. I had seen it all before and, like many wives, my insensitivity was based on my own practical experiences. Deep down in the recesses of every woman's heart and mind, in the spaces not corrupted by contrived societal notions of equality and fairness, we all secretly know these words to be true: Men are total wimps when they get sick.

Several years into our marriage, I began to notice a recurring behavioral pattern every time Francis caught a cold. Unnecessary sniffling, dramatic coughing, flamboyant sneezing. Each occurrence followed by a moan, groan, or whimper, along with a pitiable declaration such as, "I don't feel so good."

Francis's pathetic actions while sick did not appear to be natural and spontaneous. They seemed intended to garner the maximum amount of attention (also known as "milking it"). Additionally, when sick, Francis never said to me directly, "Honey, I think I'm coming down with something and would appreciate you making me some chicken soup while I take it easy for the next couple days." Instead, he put on a theatrical display in hopes of indirectly compelling me to run and get him a blankie and Fudgsicles.

Why would my otherwise responsible, straightforward, masculine military husband resort to such childish passive-aggressive tactics? I wondered.

At first I thought his germ-induced plea for attention might have something to do with having grown up in a big family. One of five siblings, Francis was flanked by the smartest kid and the funniest kid in the sibling line-up, so he had to do whatever he could to get his parents' attention.

Occurrences which most kids might avoid were savored in Francis's large family. For example, normally a child might hate going with Mom to get orthopedic shoes, a tonsillectomy, allergy testing, and speech therapy. In Francis's upbringing, however, these were precious moments, when Mom showed him special attention and bought him ice cream. Perhaps having the flu was similarly desirable.

My big family theory seemed to explain Francis's histrionic reaction to the common cold, until I started talking to other wives. Apparently, Francis wasn't the only man on the planet who exhibits attention-seeking behavior when ill.

As I watched Francis moan and groan on our couch, I wondered why I found my husband's childish ploys for attention so patently unattractive. I felt a twinge of guilt. Shouldn't my natural nurturing instincts kick in? Instead of murmuring soothing words to the sufferer, I found myself muttering insensitive remarks under my breath, such as, "He should get an Oscar for that sneeze," or "Building the groundwork for another afternoon nap, are we?" or "Grow a pair, would ya?"

I couldn't help but wonder whether my reaction might serve a higher purpose for the species. After all, if sick males were always babied by their female companions, they might start to stay home all the time instead of getting back to the work of hunting and gathering to keep the tribe strong. Maybe nature built an automatic trigger into the wifely psyche, so women would be repulsed by pathetic sickly husbands. That might motivate men to recover quickly to become attractive to women again and thereby resume their main goal in life: mating.

Later that night, Francis told me he thought he had a severe case of bronchitis and needed me to take his temperature, run to the store for cherry cough drops and ginger ale, toast him a pizza bagel, and tuck a blanket around him while he watched *South Park* reruns. I stared at him a minute with my arms crossed, rolled my eyes, and went to the kitchen to open him a can of chicken noodle soup.

It wasn't easy to ignore his hoarse pleas for more intensive care and attention, but I figured it was the least I could do for humanity.

SEASON 2 ◆ EPISODE 4

LORD OF THE HOUSEFLIES

The kids forgot to put their dishes in the dishwasher. Again.

"That's IT! If you people can't cooperate, then THIS government is shutting down!" I shouted while they stared at me from across the kitchen.

They had no idea what I was talking about, but with threats of government shutdown dominating the news that week, I just couldn't resist. Besides, threatening the kids simply felt good.

With Francis at work much of the time, I was the sole Governor of the Household. The Commander in Chief of the Homefront. The Lord of the Houseflies. I was the legislative, judicial, and executive branches all rolled up into one spatula-wielding dictator.

When the masses defied my authority, I could have, theoretically, staged a government shutdown of my own. Of course, the kids knew my threats were completely idle. Although I couldn't help but wonder: *What if it really happened?...*

The kids woke to the loud slam of Mom's bedroom door.

Peeking through the keyhole, they saw she had dragged the coffee maker, four cans of Pringles, three bottles of wine, and a boxed DVD set of Orange Is the New Black *into her room and locked the door.*

A sign taped outside read, "Government Shutdown Until

Further Notice."

The three kids—Hayden, Anna and Lilly—stared groggily at the sign for a minute. As reality dawned on them, they turned to each other and grinned.

"Cool!" Lilly exclaimed, "This is gonna be fun!"

In their pajamas, they raced to the kitchen. "I call the rest of the Cap'n Crunch!" Anna shouted, sliding across the tile floor while wearing yesterday's dirty socks.

"Forget cereal," Hayden declared, "I'm eating chocolate cake, and I might have a slice of leftover pizza for dessert!"

An hour later, the kids were stuffed and lazing the day away in front of the television, watching a marathon of Jersey Shore and sipping Coca-Cola through Pixy Stix.

However, the toilet clogged midday, the wet laundry in the washing machine started to stink, and the milk ran out. Discovering that the lunch money jar had over twenty bucks in coins, Anna exclaimed, "C'mon guys, let's go to the store—I'll make us a feast!"

Hayden stayed home for a fifth hour of Grand Theft Auto, while Lilly emerged from her room dressed in booty shorts, spaghetti string halter top, fuzzy slippers, knotted hair, and two days' worth of plaque on her teeth. "Ready!"

After their shopping trip, the girls concocted an Ovaltine aperitif accompanied by a delectable chocolate mini-doughnut amuse bouche. The entrée was a lovely microwaved trio de fromage—fried mozzarella sticks, Totino's cheese pizza, and Hot Pockets—with a generous side of tater tots.

Finding no clean utensils, they ate dessert—a scrumptious brownie chunk ice cream—straight out of the carton with used Popsicle sticks and washed it down with Red Bull.

The party raged on. Bored with Jerry Springer reruns and punching buttons on the microwave, the novelty of anarchy began to wear off around day three.

"When is Mom coming outta there?" Lilly whined.

"I don't know, but this is starting to get serious," Anna said. "My cropped jeans need to be washed, and ever since you blew a fuse microwaving that can of ravioli, my curling iron doesn't work!"

Hayden, recuperating from his video game bender, chimed in, "Yeah, and Mom needs to go to the grocery store. I actually had to eat a banana for breakfast. This is a crisis situation!"

Standing before Mom's bedroom door, the kids pounded, wailed, and made promises.

When Mom finally emerged, the kids bombard her with desperate hugs and kisses.

"Mom!" they cried, "Don't ever leave us again! We can't live without you! We promise we'll do whatever you want from now on!"

...I awoke from my daydream with a newfound sense of satisfaction. Never mind that staging my own government shutdown was complete fantasy. It had effectively convinced me that, even though my family didn't realize it, they could never live without me.

A mom can dream, can't she?

SEASON 2 ◆ EPISODE 5

VACATIONER'S DEADLIEST CATCH

Keeping the kids entertained so the adults could relax was always the primary objective during our yearly summer visits to the family beach cottage. Maz, Tray, Jacq, Francis, and I would have been perfectly happy lounging in our folding chairs every day on the beach. But the kids would only put up with so much swimming in the ocean, building sand castles, and parental relaxation. We had to be creative to find alternative activities for them and more lounging time for us.

One summer, after expensive and slightly sketchy go-kart tracks had been patronized, bug-infested mini-golf courses played, and scorching sand dunes climbed, someone suggested the last resort: crabbing. The kids loved the suspense and adventure of reeling in and scooping up dangerous crustaceans. The adults were less enthusiastic, because we knew the truth about crabbing. It's inconvenient, hot, dirty, smelly, and labor-intensive. However, we gave in, perhaps lured by the potential for relaxing in our beach chairs between catches, intervals that might be anywhere from thirty seconds to a full twenty-four-hour-and-fifty-two-minute tidal cycle.

It was a trade-off. To earn those moments of relaxation, first we had to forage for equipment: nets, long strings with sinkers and hooks tied on one end, and bait—the stinkier the better. We also needed secondary supplies: beach chairs, of course; games and books for the inevitable boredom while waiting for a bite; a first-aid kit in case of the wrong kind of bite.

Finally, we needed one cooler for cold beverages and another one for our catch. Experience taught us never to use the beverage cooler to hold the crabs, unless we wanted them marinated in Budweiser. The claws of an angry, cornered crab could pierce a beer can with one snap. Also, the convenience of lugging only one cooler was never worth the risk of severe puncture wounds when reaching in for a cold one.

Finally, we had to haul everything to a suitable dock on the bay. After setting up our chairs and unraveling our crabbing strings, we placed rotting chicken necks or fish heads firmly on each hook. We chucked the baited hooks several feet into the bay, tied the strings to the dock, then plopped into our comfy lawn chairs and opened our first round of cold beverages.

Aaah, crabbing's not so bad, we thought—briefly.

Francis caught the first crab. He felt a twitch and pulled his string ever so slowly, luring the unsuspecting crab toward the dock. When he finally saw it in the water at the end of his line, he gasped, jumped, and knocked over his beer.

"I got one! Grab the net!" he shouted.

Miraculously, he had not scared away his catch, so Maz grabbed a net to scoop up the crab as it reached the surface, while Francis yelled helpfully, "Get the damned thing, for Pete's sake!"

Unfortunately when depositing the crab in the cooler, Maz missed, and the crabby fugitive went scrambling around on the dock while the kids hopped up and down emitting blood-curdling screams.

Francis eventually got his first crab in the cooler. Now, all we had to do was repeat that feat ninety-six more times to yield enough meat to feed our family of eleven, as long as we also served corn on the cob, watermelon, bread, hamburgers, salad, beans, and plenty of desserts.

On another summer day, we were saved all these trials when a rental car pulled up to the corner outside our beach cottage. Three men got out lugging a bushel basket and began having a heated debate in another language. Sensing they were from out of town, I shouted from our deck, "You folks need some help?"

One man spoke a bit of English, and he explained they were Korean businessmen who had just returned from a chartered crabbing trip. He opened the bushel basket, revealing layer upon layer of beautiful, gurgling, blue crabs. He told us they were staying in a hotel, and unless we wanted to take the crabs off their hands, they were headed to the beach to release them.

On one hand, it would have been hilarious to watch the three well-intentioned tourists inadvertently cause utter mayhem by emptying a bushel basket of vicious crabs amongst the sunbathers at the beach. On the other hand, it's not every day that someone walks up to your deck, where you are sitting comfortably with drink in hand, and offers you sixty-bucks-worth of fresh-caught seafood for free.

Needless to say, we took the crabs off their hands, because that's the kind of generous Americans we are. Bowing and waving, they thanked us profusely for helping them out, and we shamelessly accepted their misplaced gratitude.

As the rental car pulled away, we—Tray, Jacq, Maz, Francis and I—looked blankly at each other. Our crabbing ventures had never netted a catch this size, and we all wondered just how we would manage crab preparation on a large scale.

"Okay," Tray finally said, "Let's get started cooking these things!"

Jacq found a can of Old Bay Seasoning in our spice cabinet and read from the back of the container. "Says here, fill the bottom of the pot with equal parts water and vinegar, bring to a boil, then layer the crabs in the steamer with seasoning. Cover and steam twenty to thirty minutes until the crabs turn red."

Piece of cake, we thought. As we readied our ingredients, we clinked our beers in mutual admiration of our ingenuity. We knew we were not like all the *other* beach tourists. We had a beach house and a steamer pot. We cooked our own crabs. We were practically as good as locals.

"Water's boiling!" Maz yelped, and Tray retrieved the basket of crabs from our deck, where the kids were poking them with sticks and watching them snap. As the rest of us huddled at a safe distance, Tray picked up the angry crabs with tongs and lowered them, one by one, into the deadly steam.

The kids looked on, confused. Like most kids, they loved animals, and they loved food. But they did not often witness the ruthless conversion from one to the other. Poking the crabs with sticks was one thing. Cooking them alive was another.

"It's not going to hurt, is it?" Lilly asked.

"Oh, no, they think they're taking a nice bath," Maz lied.

Just then, a crab leapt from the pot in a desperate fight for survival—or escape from his soothing final bath. As the escapee scrambled sideways toward us, Francis emitted a girlish squeal and knocked me out of the way to get onto a barstool. The kids wailed and dug their nails into each other, while Maz sprang spryly onto the couch. The rest is a little foggy, but two minutes later, our kitchen broom was broken in half, two kids were crying, I had a mysterious scratch on my shoulder, and the escaped crustacean was back in the pot.

Thankfully, the neighbors did not report the commotion to the local police. Despite the brouhaha, the crabs were steamed to perfection. Our mouths watered in anticipation of what would surely be a quintessential summer vacation meal.

We piled the hot crabs in the center of our newspaper-covered table and surrounded the pile with lemon wedges and bowls of melted butter. We trustingly gave each kid a wooden mallet and turned them loose on the steamed crabs. We reminded them how to crack the crabs to get to the meat, not bothering to identify unappetizing parts like gills, intestines, and genitals. Regardless of the arguably revolting nature of crab cracking and picking, the kids were so caught up in the fun of pounding their mallets, they didn't notice. With each strike, the kids squealed as shell fragments flew and crab juice squirted.

For at least two hours, the eleven of us hammered and cracked, plucked and dipped, until every morsel of crab meat from that gift bushel had been extracted and consumed.

"I am exhausted!" Francis exclaimed once all the crabs were picked and eaten.

"Well, I hope you're not too tired of picking," I replied, "because you'll have to pick a place to order pizza when everyone starts complaining that they're still hungry."

SEASON 2 ◆ EPISODE 6

THANKSGIVING'S
FORBIDDEN FRUIT

Every Thanksgiving, Francis announces proudly that the stuffing was his favorite part of the meal. Invariably, Anna loved the sweet potatoes, and Lilly went gaga over the mashed potatoes. Hayden couldn't get enough of the turkey.

But I was usually too embarrassed to admit my favorite Thanksgiving dish. Ever since I was a kid, I didn't do cartwheels over eating turkey. I didn't drool over the mashed potatoes or my father's giblet gravy. I didn't love, or even like for that matter, those miniature pickles and whatnots on my mother's sectioned relish tray. I thought the stuffing had too many unidentifiable objects in it to be palatable, and I wouldn't even touch a yam, candied or otherwise. Believe it or not, I never got jazzed up about the pumpkin pie, even with a humongous dollop of Cool Whip.

My favorite part of my family's Thanksgiving meal was the one that sat in a little pressed glass dish at the corner of the dining table. It didn't require much preparation, but it was an essential part of our feast that I looked forward to every year: canned cranberry sauce.

In the seventies, my family ate everything out of cans. Peas, corn, fruit juice, grapefruit sections, ham, chow mein, beef stew, liverwurst, even chocolate syrup. We celebrated ingenious cooking short cuts, including processed meats, flavored gelatin, and mini marshmallows. Back then, canned cranberry sauce was downright trendy in our neighborhood. And delicious.

When I was old enough to use the can opener, my mother let me prepare the cranberries for our Thanksgiving meal. After I released the suction and pried off the lid, the jellied cylinder would slide right out onto the pressed glass dish with a pleasing little plop, perfectly intact and still showing the ridged impressions of the can. Using a table knife, I'd slowly carve the rounded mold into uniform disks that wiggled as I carried them to the table.

The smooth, translucent slices glowed like rubies in the candlelight refracting through the glass dish. We passed it around like a cherished chalice, delving delicate slices of sweet tanginess with a silver spoon.

Back then, a can of cranberry sauce cost less than a quarter, but it tasted divine. A plate of traditional fare—turkey, stuffing, sweet potatoes and corn—was most definitely refined by a slice of glimmering cranberry sauce. It gave our Thanksgiving dinner elevated status and made it seem gourmet, fancy, high-class.

After marrying Francis and sharing Thanksgiving dinners with military friends from all over, I found out not everyone shares my taste for canned cranberry sauce.

"You make your own cranberry sauce, right?" friends would ask.

And to save face, I would lie. "Oh, of course! I always make cranberry sauce from scratch, you know, with the real cranberries and, uh...the sugar and...uh, what's that other ingredient?"

Even though I've learned how to make cranberry sauce from scratch, I never let a Thanksgiving go by without sneaking a smack of my beloved canned version, and I've passed the task of plopping and slicing on to my children. To me, canned cranberry sauce represents an edible virtue, a life lesson, a sweet reminder that no matter how times or circumstances change, I should always be myself.

SEASON 2 ◆ EPISODE 7

WANTED: MOM MANAGER

I was late for the meeting as usual.

With an armful of crumpled papers, I rushed down the hall. Sheepishly, I found a seat at the table, and began with as much authority as I could muster:

"This meeting is called to order at, let's see, twelve minutes after nine. If you don't mind, I'd prefer that these weekly sessions start promptly at the top of the hour. Now, without further delay, let's get down to business."

"The van still needs new brakes, and if you wait much longer, you'll be paying for rotors too. You volunteered to bring snacks to Hayden's flag football game on Tuesday at 3:15, but you must somehow get Lilly to the dentist at four o'clock. The checkbook hasn't been balanced in three months, which might explain why you bounced a check last week," I continued.

"Francis is on his last pair of clean underwear, so please put a load of hot whites in at your earliest convenience. Moby is due for his monthly flea and tick medication. You have two articles due this week. The repairman is coming on Thursday between eight and two to fix the fridge. And you need to get serious about that juice cleanse. Now, how do you plan to get all that done?" I finished and took a slurp of coffee.

Crickets.

No one responded because I was having my weekly meeting with myself, and as usual I had no idea how to answer my own demands. I scribbled a to-do list, marked a few things on the calendar, and then went about my day, determined to get it all done once and for all.

But deep inside, I knew the inevitable pattern of my life would repeat itself. My week would start out productive. Something would throw me off track—a car repair, a sick kid, writer's block. One item on my list would collide into the next, and the ensuing pile up would become overwhelming.

By Friday, Francis would come home from work to find no dinner, unfolded laundry heaped on the coffee table, and me, dazed and unshowered, draped over my computer chair where I'd been surfing vintage ceramic Christmas trees on eBay for three hours.

What fundamental flaw in my character made it so difficult for me to keep up with my responsibilities as a mom?

After some thought, fueled by half a box of Cheese Nips, I realized I have always been a soldier, not a commander. A worker bee, not the queen. I'm not lazy. I'm not incompetent. I'm not disorganized. I just need a supervisor, a boss, a manager to watch over me and keep me on track.

Ahh, how different things would be with someone to offer clear direction and guidance.

"Ms. Molinari," my manager might say, "While it is clear that you are no stranger to hard work, there is room for improvement in the areas of task prioritization, self-motivation, and personal hygiene. It is my recommendation that you avoid distractions from your daily priorities such as online shopping, free samples, and midday reruns of *Lost*."

But unless I found a manager willing to be compensated in meatloaf, I couldn't afford to pay someone to give me direction and motivation.

I am the manager, damn it, and I have to take responsibility, I thought. *Even if it feels like I'm being dragged through life behind my dirty white minivan, I'll continue this never-ending game of catch-up until the job is done. I'll try to avoid getting tangled in the particulars—the emails, the dust bunnies, the bills, the burnt dinners, the dark roots—and focus on the big picture: keeping our family happy and healthy.*

Fortunately, long-term analysis indicated the family was on an upward trend. Subordinates still complained from time to time, but overall they reported excellent workplace satisfaction. As manager, I sometimes lacked efficiency, but I made it up in dedication, sincerity, and willingness to work overtime and on weekends without pay.

Despite its flaws, our family business was thriving, so I could see no immediate need for new management.

Meeting adjourned.

SEASON 2 ◆ EPISODE 8

HOW MANY IDIOTS DOES IT TAKE TO FILL OUT A 1040?

"Oh crud, we need to do our taxes," I groaned to Francis, as I did every April.

After exhausting every reason to procrastinate—cleaning out the crisper drawer in the fridge, perusing old Hickory Farms catalogs left over from Christmas, clipping toenails, surfing eBay for vintage bar signs, and napping—it's finally time to face the music.

Coffee and a folder of haphazardly collected paperwork in hand, Francis and I reluctantly plopped down in front of our computer to complete the dreaded annual tax forms.

We haven't had the best luck preparing our tax forms over the years and are conditioned to avoid the experience. Despite my law degree and Francis's master's degree in finance, we've always struggled to grasp the simple concepts relevant to our personal income tax forms.

In law school, I took a tax law course and could write a scholarly paper on whether the federal income tax is a direct tax or an excise tax based on the Sixteenth Amendment and the Supreme Court's opinion in the Pollock case. But somehow, I struggled with my 1040-EZ.

Francis's master's thesis at the Naval Postgraduate School was titled "Congress, Defense, and the Deficit: An Analysis of the FY

1996 Budget Process in the 104th Congress," but he couldn't tell the difference between short- and long-term capital gains if his retirement pay depended on it.

But still every year, we begrudgingly spread out our paperwork and somehow fulfill our annual obligation as taxpayers.

For several years, we used TurboTax, a supposedly idiot-proof program that led us through a simplified series of questions designed to accurately calculate all income and deductions.

Somehow, Francis and I were still totally confused.

"Do we qualify for the child tax credit?" I asked, as Francis slurped his coffee.

"Heck if I know. Just do whatever we did last year. That seemed to work," he said nonchalantly.

"I forget, do we have Roth IRAs or regular IRAs?" I said a few minutes later. Rifling through a pile of papers, Francis found our statements, which might as well have been written in Chinese.

"Roth, but what on earth is a 'recharacterized contribution'?"

My eyes started to cross as I tried to decipher our mutual fund papers. "Is 'cost basis' the same as 'purchase price'?" I said, searching my faded memory bank.

"I don't know. Just punch in two hundred dollars and see what happens," Francis suggested.

After four hours, two pots of coffee, three calls to our financial manager, and at least a dozen choice expletives, we finally keyed all the numbers in and dutifully sent our forms off to Uncle Sam.

We didn't get our refund check for several weeks, but by then we'd already spent it and lost the receipt. When our bank statements arrived, we didn't balance the checkbook. And we knew that by the following April, we'd be back in front of our computer, dazed and confused all over again.

SEASON 2 ◆ EPISODE 9

BIRDS, BEES, AND BRATS

"Time for gelato!" I blurted, pulling our kids away from a statue at the Vatican Museum during a family trip to Rome. We had stopped on our way to the Sistine Chapel to take a closer look at the strange female sculpture we initially thought was covered in some kind of fruit. Were they mangoes?

The plaque on the adjacent wall explained she was Artemis, the goddess of fertility, and she was adorned with severed bull testicles.

Ahem.

While stationed in Europe, Francis and I tried to expose Hayden, Anna, and Lilly to art, history, and culture as much as possible. This might qualify as overexposure.

Typical military brats, our kids had no idea how fortunate they were to live a minivan ride away from Paris, Berlin, Vienna, Florence, Amsterdam, Barcelona, Prague, and other European cultural meccas. Sometimes to their chagrin, we took them to see paintings and sculptures in every city we visited.

And, as it is with art, many of the renderings were explicit, causing our children to giggle, gawk, or grimace in embarrassment. We indulged them—they are kids, after all—and hoped someday when it mattered, they'd remember standing before the original works of Manet, Michelangelo, Klimt, Matisse, Botticelli,

Cezanne, Donatello, and other greats.

However, some pieces were so detailed, they caused our children's mental wheels to spin.

Wait a minute... what is that, and what's it for anyway?

After fielding many awkward questions, Francis and I got good at knowing which masterpieces we should breeze by quickly.

We shuffled the kids past explicit nudes in Paris's Musée D'Orsay on our way to see classics like Monet's *Blue Water Lilies* and *Whistler's Mother*. We didn't let the kids linger too long at the base of Giambologna's *The Rape of Sabines* in Florence's Galleria dell'Accademia, opting instead to find Michelangelo's anatomically humongous but relatively benign *David*.

Often, as we did when we realized the statue of Artemis in the Vatican was not covered in mangoes after all, we used the oldest diversion in the book—ice cream. However, on our final European excursion before moving back to the States, it became clear I could no longer avoid the curiosity of our youngest child, Lilly.

We were nearing the end of our three years of living in Germany. Francis had already moved to his next duty station at Naval Station Mayport, Florida, and I stayed behind so the kids could finish out the school year. Regretting that we'd never had the chance to visit Greece and Croatia, I booked a last-minute cruise with ports of call in Venice, Bari, Corfu, and Dubrovnik.

"Perfect!" I thought, looking forward to checking the rest of the boxes on my family's travel wish list. But of course, things were not perfect.

Lilly, Anna, and I got seasick after departing Venice. After a long night of tag-teaming in our state room's tiny bathroom and rationing the remaining scraps of toilet paper, we wandered around Bari the following morning, dazed and queasy. In my weakened state, I didn't have the energy to censor what the kids were seeing. All I could do was sip shakily from a cappuccino while they gawked at nude statues and giggled at paintings.

I could tell that Lilly's head was spinning with questions.

Later, while Anna and Hayden visited the arcade, I took Lilly for a mother-daughter dinner at the ship's buffet. Even though my parental judgment was still somewhat impaired from lingering seasickness, I decided to seize the opportunity to enlighten my daughter.

Sitting there in a booth on that Italian cruise ship, using breadsticks and rigatoni noodles as my visual aids, I told Lilly all about the birds and the bees.

Too stunned to finish her pasta, Lilly just sat there, her brown eyes wide. It was as if she was trying to process all she had seen during our three years in Europe. Whether this bombshell made things easier or more difficult for her to comprehend, I couldn't say.

All I knew was, if Lilly asked me any follow up questions, I was armed with the perfect answer—"Let's get some ice cream!"

SEASON 2 ◆ EPISODE 10

WAR OF THE ROSES

It was a night like any other night.

The soft glow of the television winked off, signaling the start of our bedtime ritual. I hoisted my weary body out of its hollow in our sofa and began my journey down the hall to our bedroom, flicking off lights and peeking into the kids' rooms on the way. Francis peeled himself out of his leather recliner and plodded off to the kitchen to set the coffee maker to brew the hot elixir that would awaken us in eight hours.

Peering into my baggy eyes in our bathroom mirror, I flossed, brushed, and gulped down a self-prescribed combination of eight vitamins, minerals, essential oils, and fiber, intended to keep me eternally young. And regular.

Although he used to simply strip down to his undies and hop into bed, Francis joined me at our double sinks, to floss and brush his teeth, including a recently filled molar.

With oral hygiene completed, we fumbled into our bedclothes and climbed into bed, I on his right, and he on my left.

"Hike," Francis commanded with his eyes already closed. I obliged, lifting my left leg and flopping it over his right. With our legs intertwined in such a way, we kissed goodnight and silence fell.

"Hey, you're over the roses," I murmured.

Our bed, a hundred-year-old French antique with three roses carved into the apex of its lovely arched headboard, was only wide enough for a full-sized mattress. The middle rose had always been our equator, our 38th parallel, our Berlin Wall.

Despite our substantial frames, we had been sleeping on this full-sized mattress our entire marriage, and territorial disputes arose frequently.

With a loud "tsk," Francis jerked his girth two inches to the left. As I waited for the resulting undulations of the bed to subside, I opened my book.

"The light!" Francis moaned. I turned off the overhead light, fumbled for my book light and turned it on.

"Holy cow, that thing is bright," he whined. He dragged a pillow over his eyes, and I compromised by angling the beam away from his side of the bed.

A few minutes later, a familiar sound interrupted my reading. It was a rhythmic racket like sandpaper scraping rough wood, always accompanied by a prolonged jiggling of the mattress. These well-known clues pointed to only one thing: Francis was scratching himself again.

When we lived in moister climates, his scratching was incessant, and often included the additional disruption of him furiously rubbing his burning feet together. Although I offered various creams and powders in hopes of dousing his fiery itch, Francis never seemed to mind. In fact, he took pride in the association of his condition with "jocks" and "athletes."

The sounds and shakes soon subsided, topped off with a loud, prolonged yawn. Silence returned, and my mind wandered back to the pages of my book. I lost myself in the wordy descriptions of the characters and began to doze.

Onions. My eyelids blinked open and I turned my head to the left. In the dim light, I saw Francis's open mouth about six inches from my face. I crinkled my nose at the hot breath emanating from this seemingly enormous, dark cave.

Interestingly, the smell of Francis's breath bore no relation to his eating habits. I didn't recall serving the aromatic bulb with dinner or dessert for that matter, but somehow his mouth was giving off the clear scent of onions. The same irrational rules governed the odor of his belches. I could serve him a heaping plate of sugar cookies, and if he burped afterward, it would smell like salami. Go figure.

"Hon, could you face the other direction?" I gingerly suggested. It took him a sleepy second to process my request, and then he smacked his dry lips, growled, and repositioned onto his back with a tuck and jerk motion.

With our bed finally still, silent, and free of noxious odors, I surrendered to slumber.

My eyelids twitched, as my dreams turned fitful. With a tiny gasp, I awakened and realized the growling wolf in my dreams was my snoring husband. "Honey, turn on your *other* side," I whispered.

"Huh? Whah?" he mumbled. With another "tsk" of exasperation, he jerked and tucked his body to the left, managing to curl our entire quilt around himself like a giant burrito.

I lay awake a few minutes, thinking of our nightly ritual and whether or not it indicated anything about our relationship. I felt remorse for making Francis accommodate my light-sleep habits, and contemplated spooning him to communicate my regret.

"Hike," Francis whispered knowingly from his side of the roses. I flopped my leg back over his. Warm and secure in our little bed, we happily drifted off to sleep.

SEASON 2 ◆ EPISODE 11

THE STUFF FAMILIES
ARE MADE OF

I was told that my family of five weighed nearly eighteen thousand pounds.

No, we were not morbidly obese—that figure was actually the estimated total weight of all our stuff, according to our military movers. Everything from the half-chewed pencil in the desk drawer to the 1978 Baldwin upright piano, and all the socks, cookie sheets, end tables, and dog toys in between.

We were about to make the move from Germany to another duty station, this time Naval Station Mayport, Florida. But before the team of movers arrived to wrap all our stuff in paper, pack it into boxes, nail it into crates, weigh it, and deliver it to our next temporary home, we had to take some time to sort through our eighteen thousand pounds of stuff and purge unnecessary items like old clothes, outgrown toys, and beat-up furniture.

Getting rid of things has always been difficult for me. As a child, I used to squirrel everything away—toys, coins, rocks, shells, candy, notes, photos—and I still do it as an adult. I can attach practical or sentimental value to almost anything to make it worth keeping.

Before we packed for our move from England to Virginia, Francis was going through all the little drawers in his big roll top desk and came upon a small white plastic clamp holding a small, brownish object.

"What the heck is this?" he asked, holding the clamp up to the light.

"Oh, that's Hayden's umbilical cord," I said, briefly looking up from a file box of bank statements.

"His umbilical cord?!" he said, astonished, tossing the dehydrated fragment back into the drawer. "That looks like something you'd find in a bowl of Chex Mix...what if I'd accidentally eaten it? I'm throwing it away."

"Wait!" I shouted, lunging for the dried-up morsel. I held the plastic clamp and gazed at the petrified remnants of the bridge of flesh that once connected my son and me. I thought of the life-giving nourishment that flowed through the cord and how it symbolized our undying love.

Francis interrupted my reverie.

"Hon, you're not going to keep that thing, are you?"

As I reluctantly threw the scabby scrap into the trash, I wondered whether discarding the original physical bond between my son and me might adversely affect our emotional ties.

I knew it was crazy, yet I went through the same insane thought processes with every move.

I couldn't give in to believing every scrap of paper and old shoe was indispensable because it held some dear memory or might come in handy one day. If I did, we'd easily exceed the military's weight limit for moving a family of five. Uncle Sam's discipline kept me from becoming a true hoarder, but I still battled my inner packrat every time he ordered us to move.

I hesitated over a restaurant matchbook from a night when the kids didn't embarrass us. I had trouble parting with my 1980s Bermuda bag and its buttoned covers, convinced that preppy wooden-handled purses might come back into style. And I couldn't get myself to part with the tin drum my son used to beat when we went Christmas caroling with the neighbors.

With each move, I had to remind myself that, although our stuff comforted us and made us feel at home in unfamiliar places, the eighteen thousand pounds of stuff following us around the world did not make us who we were.

Without it we still had a hefty family life—weighty with memories, loaded with laughter, and laden with love.

SEASON THREE

IN THE TRENCHES

SEASON 3 ◆ EPISODE 1

MIDDLE SCHOOL DISORIENTATION

My daughters and I nervously passed between two huge concrete lions flanking the entrance, and a door opened magically before us.

"Welcome to Julia Landon College Preparatory School!" said the eighth grader holding the door, smartly clad in khaki shorts, a navy-blue polo emblazoned with the school logo, and a full set of shining braces.

It was middle school orientation day, and having just moved to Jacksonville, Florida, from our previous duty station in Germany, we had no clue how to negotiate the vast halls and complex social hierarchy of this new institution.

With every move, our military family adapted to new surroundings, but this time we were a bit anxious. Anna and Lilly had been accepted into the area's top magnet middle school, and while I was grateful for this stroke of luck, I was also a bit worried I might meet up with some pretentious personalities.

Being from humble roots, I tended to become self-conscious when I perceived that people were snooty.

I believed middle school parents were a separate and distinct breed, because they were still living the dream that their children would grow up to be the cream of the crop. Unlike elementary school children who were more of a blank canvas, and high school kids whose personalities were pretty much set, middle school children were hovering in the middle—still forming their individual aptitudes and character traits. Middle school parents still believed that, with their guidance, their children would become neurosurgeons, famous artists, or professional athletes.

I had a sneaking suspicion that the parents at Julia Landon College Preparatory School might have cornered the market on elitist attitudes, so I decided to beat them at their own game.

I knew I needed to walk into that school wearing something that would convey the message, "I'm new, I'm smart, I'm interesting, and I have no time for you."

So, I strategically paired a trendy shirtdress with a silver pendant necklace on a leather cord. I carried one of those huge tote bags with the name of a European city stamped all over it. Mine read "Stuttgart."

I envisioned another mom asking, "Ooh, cool necklace... where'd you get it?" and I'd have to tell how I bought the pendant from a street market in Rome after a delicious lunch of risotto and fried artichokes in a Trastevere café. I'd have that far-away look in my eye that says, "I've got more culture in my upturned pinkie than you'd get from a case of Chobani."

Then someone else might notice my Stuttgart bag and inquire as to whether I have "visited" Germany. I'd have to hide my smirk as I explain, "Why, no, actually we *lived* in Stuttgart for the last three years." Again, with that far-away look in my eyes.

That'll show 'em, I thought, as we crossed the threshold into the school.

We were greeted by more khaki-clad kids, each one more polite and helpful than the last, "Yes ma'am" rolling off their tongues without the slightest effort.

I grumbled under my breath at their superiority.

I'd been trying to get Hayden, Anna, and Lilly to use that simple phrase for years, but even under extreme duress I had only been able to elicit a reluctant muttering that sounded more like "S'pam." Apparently my kids would rather shove Popsicle sticks under their toenails than subordinate themselves in such a humiliating way. I preferred to not be referred to as a canned-meat product, so I gave up the fight and accepted the garden variety "Yes, Mom," usually accompanied by plenty of eye rolling.

We followed the sea of people headed to several stations set up for getting locker assignments, student ID photos, PTA memberships, textbooks, and PE uniforms. The crowd looked like a giant preppy wave of madras plaid, nautical stripes, tanned limbs, sun-bleached hair, and white teeth. Parents seemed to recognize each other, chatting as the tide swept forward.

In a pathetic ploy for attention, I announced at each station, "We are new here," but no one seemed to care all that much. They were as pleasant as eating a slice of summer peach pie on a porch swing. But I wasn't about to let these sweet-tea swilling snobs get the best of me.

In a last-ditch effort to get the upper hand, I announced to the silver-haired guidance counselor, "Well, you see, we are new because WE JUST MOVED HERE AFTER LIVING IN EUROPE," hoping the surrounding crowd would overhear and drop to their knees to beg for my friendship.

But strangely, no one batted an eye.

In her slow-cooked southern drawl, the guidance counselor responded, "Well, I do declare, you have come a long way! Welcome, we are so happy to have you here. Now, how may I help you?"

Contritely, I handed the sweet woman Anna's and Lilly's health records and thanked her for her assistance. I couldn't deny it any more. The people at this new school weren't snooty or elitist. I didn't need to beat them at their own game, because they weren't playing one. With a sigh of relief, I finally let down my guard and resolved to just be real.

As I walked back out the door and between the concrete lions, I remembered the advice I had given Anna and Lilly that very morning: "Don't be afraid, just be yourself. In time, you'll make lots of new friends and fit right in."

Point taken.

SEASON 3 ◆ EPISODE 2

BATTLE OF THE BULGE

One busy weeknight while chewing the last bites of pork chops and boxed macaroni and cheese, I asked Francis, "Did I tell you about my conversation with the sixth-grade math teacher today?"

Gnawing a particularly tough piece of meat, Francis shook his head with a familiar glazed look in his eyes. After nearly two decades of marriage, he knew I could take a good twenty minutes to describe cleaning the fuzz out of the lint trap, so he settled into his seat and braced himself for excruciating detail and superfluous analysis.

"Well, I called him about the semester project," I continued, "and do you know what he said?"

"No. What?" Francis robotically replied, staring blankly into space.

I went on, in great detail, to describe a mundane event in my daily life as a stay-at-home mother of three. Many years of housewifery had taught me I could give our regular dinner conversation a stimulating dose of drama and suspense if I merely embellished my otherwise ordinary stories with exhaustive descriptions, exaggerated voice intonation, and vivid facial expressions.

I told Francis all about my phone call with the math teacher, imbuing it with the zest of a thrilling off-Broadway play. During a particularly expressive point in my story Francis, tired and irritated after a long day and a mediocre dinner, interjected sardonically, "Oh, please, do that again with the bulgy eyes. That's *really* attractive."

Fully intending to add insult to injury, he mocked me by imitating my Marty Feldman expression, while I sat, stone-faced, glaring at him.

Although his deep-set eyeballs could never mimic the natural prominence of mine, Francis nonetheless contorted his face to look as ridiculous as possible. As I watched his discourteous display and doggedly gripped my fork over our weeknight dinner, our entire marriage flashed before my genetically protuberant eyes.

What's happened to us? I wondered. *We used to be so lovey-dovey, and now we're pelting each other with insults over Shake 'n Bake! Is our marriage hopeless? Does he think I've become unattractive and annoying? But wait just a minute, here....I don't recall anyone dying and making him God's gift to women. Harrumph!*

Bitter, I finally interrupted his facial contortions. "So, who do you think you are over there, Robert Redford or something?"

With blatant hypocrisy, Francis took immediate offense to my sarcasm and scowled.

We sat in silence, sucking the macaroni from our teeth and avoiding eye contact.

Unable to remain mute for more than a minute, I spoke weakly without looking up from my plate. "I can't help that my eyes bulge, you know."

Francis's irritation was suddenly replaced with remorse. "Oh, Honey, I'm sorry," he said, moving in closer and placing his hand on mine. "I don't think your eyes bulge. I think you're bulgy in all the right places."

His awkward flattery softened my ire, and I released the death grip I had on my fork. Glancing up from the remains of my pork chop and into Francis's deep-set eyes, I thought, "I only have eyes for you, dear ... whether you like it or not."

SEASON 3 ◆ EPISODE 3

THE CAR POOL BLUES

I get up early in the mornin', round about six o'clock.
Bleary-eyed and yawnin', I gather up the flock.
Three chillins in the van, we drive around the block.
At the neighbor's crib, two are added to my stock.

Coffee cup in hand, I head for open road.
My minivan groans under such a heavy load.
Been doin' this so long, I fear I might explode.
Can't blame nobody else for seeds that I have sowed.

So here I sit each morning, radio a-blarin'.
In my rear-view mirror, I see the kids a-starin'.
The high price of gasoline has tempers a-flarin'.
Bite my tongue so kids won't hear me a-swearin'.

The drive to school each mornin' is pretty much the same.
Starts out kinda quiet, inadequate sleep to blame.
Getting up so early seems such a crying shame.
Without a break on weekends, I might just go insane.

Where to tune the radio dial, no one can agree.
The girls like the latest hits on Radio Disney.

The boys say pop music is so bourgeoisie.
They prefer the screeching sounds of rock melodies.

My son, he doesn't speak, because he's fast asleep.
In five months of car-pooling, he hasn't uttered a peep.
I've often wondered if he might be counting sheep.
Into his open mouth, a bug or two might leap.

After twenty miles or so, and a dozen traffic lights,
We arrive at school on time, the sun now burning bright.
I bid them all adieu, as they scramble from my sight.
And breathe a sigh of relief—we made it there all right.

The *Slam!* of the van's door ends child domination.
Reaching for the dashboard, I switch the radio station.
Hoping news will distract me from my degradation.
Sipping dregs of tepid coffee, I grope for relaxation.

In thirty minutes, I am home, and go about my day.
Sweep the floors, walk the dog, what's for lunch today?
In no time flat, it seems to me, the hours have slipped away.
Must drive back to school again, no time for delay.

Back in the van and on the road, the blues they pervade.
I wonder, am I a lousy chauffeur who works without pay?
At home, have I become a lowly scullery maid?
I realize, there is no use for my bitter tirade.

Like tiny escaped prisoners, the kids burst out of school.
In the van I hear their chatter about who is super-cool.
I ask about their homework, if they've learned the Golden Rule.
But they're soon asleep, open mouths begin to drool.

Pulling in the driveway, they look like the walking dead.
Zombies stumble from my van, toward our humble homestead.
They search for salty snacks, and a place to lay their heads.
After homework, dinner and play, it's time to go to bed.

Five months down, five more to go, not sure if I can make it.
I worry that I'll lose my mind, if I am forced to take it.
But these kids are mine, it's true, and nothing will forsake it.
And so I must continue on, even if I fake it.

I'll try to avoid the pitfalls, like gambling and booze.
I'll remember, parenting is something that we choose.
I'll face the fact that in life, one must pay the dues.
And suffer the trials and tribulations of The Carpool Blues.

SEASON 3 ◆ EPISODE 4

LILLY SAVES CHRISTMAS

Throughout their sisterhood, Anna and Lilly had clearly defined roles, or at least Anna did. She was the boss. All Lilly had to do was follow orders, which she was usually more than happy to do. Lilly's birth ushered in Anna's reign as social director, camp counselor, master manipulator, benevolent queen, or evil dictator, depending upon her mood. Her sovereignty had only one loyal subject—her little sister—but that was enough, at least for a time, to satisfy Anna's desire for world domination.

Lilly accepted this lot in life without question or complaint. Nowhere were the contrasts in this relationship more clear than the year Lilly saved Christmas.

But first a little history. Back when we were living in Germany, Anna was the first of our three kids to deny Santa's existence. Lying in bed on Christmas Eve, she heard a noise. Thinking it was Santa, she climbed down from her top bunk to peek through the keyhole in her bedroom door into the family room, expecting to see the jolly old elf himself.

What Anna witnessed at ten years old would squash her sugar plum visions and devour her gum drop dreams. There was no man in a red suit. Instead, it was only her dad, setting out gifts under our tree.

Her mind raced with the implications of this bombshell.

Seeking comfort, she climbed into the bottom bunk with eight-year-old Lilly, who was fast asleep.

"Lilly," she whispered.

Squinting, Lilly croaked, "Whah, huh?"

"We're going to sing Christmas carols now," Anna demanded.

"Okay," said Lilly groggily but willingly, as though waking up in the middle of the night to sing Christmas carols made perfect sense.

Anna snaked her arms around Lilly's little torso, hugging her tightly for her own solace, and began in a whisper, "Silent night, holy night..." Lilly did not know all the words, but she followed Anna's lead, as usual. With their heads resting forehead to forehead on Lilly's pillow, they sang the song over and over in the dark until Anna fell into a fitful sleep.

Three years later, when we were stationed in Florida, Lilly would turn the tables on her sister, as only Lilly could do. On that Christmas Eve, once again Anna and Lilly decided to sleep together, this time in Lilly's double bed.

Watching her little sister merrily playing a Santa Claus-themed game on her Kindle, Anna grimaced. She was irritated that Lilly, at eleven years old, still believed in Santa Claus while Anna's fun had been spoiled by what she saw through the keyhole three Christmas Eves before.

She's probably faking it, Anna thought.

"You know he's not real, right?" she said to Lilly.

Lilly looked over at her big sister, confused.

"Who's not real?"

"Santa," Anna said with cold indifference. "The parents made him up, you know."

Lilly's face contorted, and her eyes welled with tears. Anna went into detail, callously explaining that the bites taken out of the carrots and cookies were taken by Dad, not Santa and his reindeer. The curly script on the packages was all written by Mom.

"Anna, you're mean!" Lilly cried, "That's wrong! None of that is true! You're just stupid!"

Rather than acknowledge any culpability for crushing her sister's Christmas psyche, Anna did what she had always done when she made a mistake—she blamed Lilly.

"Lilly!" Anna scolded, "You shouldn't talk to me like that! Say you're sorry!"

Lilly's anger transformed immediately into contrition, and she apologized.

"I just can't understand why you treat me this way," Anna replied, folding her arms and rolling to the other side of the bed to sulk.

"Please Anna, I'm sorry for saying you're stupid," Lilly pleaded. "Please forgive me!" After repeated pleas, Anna finally granted partial absolution to Lilly, so they could both get some sleep.

The next morning, Lilly being Lilly, she didn't want her new-found knowledge about the existence of Santa Claus to put a damper on the festivities. Lilly didn't say a word about it; instead she bounded down the steps and into the living room in her new fleece pajamas, grinning from ear to ear.

"Santa came!" she exclaimed, stretching her arms out wide. She got to work, doling out presents for each of us. After a significant pile of wrapping paper had accumulated in the center of the living room, and all the gifts were opened, Lilly found another present tucked behind the table that held our small, artificial tree.

"What's this?" she said, "It says it's for me from Santa!" Lilly tore the poorly wrapped gift open, revealing a small stuffed animal, a cow. Lilly hugged the fuzzy bovine and beamed, "I love it!"

I couldn't remember wrapping that gift and assumed it must've been something Francis had picked up. Conversely,

Francis assumed I had bought it. Either way, everyone was enjoying the Christmas spirit. Now that our work was done, and the kids were happy, we were both too cozy and contented to care where the cow came from.

Both girls were in college before we heard the whole story of what Anna told Lilly on that Christmas Eve and the origin of the mysterious cow. Lilly also said she'd noticed I had been struggling to get into the holidays after our move to Florida that year. She was right, the warm Christmastime weather was a difficult adjustment for me, a sad contrast to the idyllic snowy seasons of my childhood and our previous assignments. I couldn't face picking out a tree and lugging it home on a hot, humid day. Thinking the kids wouldn't notice the difference, I plumped for a four-foot fake tree instead of the large, real tree we usually had. I was wrong. Lilly noticed.

In spite of her disappointment about the tree and Anna's revelation about Santa—or perhaps because of them—Lilly was determined to bring Christmas magic back to our family. She told us she was the one who wrapped up the cow—which she had recently bought for herself—and hid it under the table, hoping we would all believe in Santa again. And for a while, we did. Maybe we still do.

Sweet, unselfish, people-pleasing Lilly reminded us the true spirit of Christmas is in the giving. She gave us a gift by giving one to herself.

SEASON 3 ◆ EPISODE 5

BATTERY BY BLENDER

"MOLINARI!" the ER nurse roared, jolting us out of our waiting room stupor. Tearing our eyes from hypnotic crime show reruns playing on the wall-mounted television, Francis and I scrambled to move twelve-year-old Lilly, who'd been placed in a wheelchair to elevate her lacerated foot.

"So, what happened?" the nurse asked.

"It was the blender," I blurted, nervously.

"The blender?!" The nurse looked in horror at Lilly's foot, wrapped in a dishtowel.

"Well, no, her foot wasn't actually in the blender…it was on the floor…and the blender was in the freezer."

"In the freezer?" the nurse asked, confused.

"I…it was me…," I mumbled culpably. "I put the glass pitcher in the freezer. When my daughter opened the door, it fell out and cut her foot."

"Ah," the nurse seemed relieved to not be dealing with a frappè-ed foot. "Let's take a quick look." As our daughter winced and whined, we carefully unraveled the dishtowel. "Hmmm…looks like you're going to need a few stitches, young lady."

The nurse fired off questions at us—"full name, date of birth, address, phone number, insurance carrier, policy number"—while tapping away at her computer.

Then, after a pregnant pause, she looked intently at us and carefully enunciated, "Has your daughter ever had stitches before?"

"No," I answered immediately.

My mind waffled, and my eyes darted.

Should I tell her about that face plant Lilly did into the side of the backyard playset? If I don't mention that, will she think I've got something to hide? Why is she asking this question anyway? Does she think we're abusive parents with a history of suspicious ER visits? I guess the whole blender story does sound a bit suspect, and I was the one who put it in the freezer to begin with. I should've known it would slide off that bag of chicken tenders! It was my fault! I'm sure the nurse is alerting the police right now! I think I hear sirens!

"Sit tight in the waiting room. When the doctor is ready for you, we'll get you all fixed up," the nurse said with a smile.

We settled back into the waiting room, just in time to see Matlock render a withering cross examination. Stagnating under the unforgiving fluorescent lights for another hour, we reassured Lilly, analyzed the people around us, leafed through dog-eared magazines, and watched an episode of *Hill Street Blues*.

Just as I thought cobwebs were forming, our name was called.

The x-ray technician, the billing rep, the nurse, the doctor—they all asked the same questions. First a battery of rapid-fire queries regarding tedious details were launched in robotic succession, followed by one carefully worded question delivered police-interrogation style.

I can't recall if the final question was "Has your daughter had stitches before?" or "Are you the abusive parent who negligently put the blender in the freezer sideways?" I prayed they wouldn't bring up Anna and Hayden, who've had their share of emergency room visits. Three broken bones, two pulled elbows, and at least a dozen stitches, with such typical excuses—fell off the couch, fell off the playset, fell into the playset, fell down the stairs. It all sounded so textbook, I was sure the police were on their way to haul me off to jail.

But finally, after three hours of waiting and thirty minutes of treatment, we were released. Feeling like some kind of middle-aged jailbird, I sheepishly wheeled Lilly back through the ER entrance.

Suddenly, "YOU'RE UNDER ARREST!" blared from the waiting room. I considered bolting, but I was still a little sore from my body sculpting class, and besides, I would need to pack my fiber pills and contour pillow before I could lead a life on the run. Just as I turned to face the wall and spread 'em, I noticed that the order had come from CHiPs Officer "Ponch" Poncherello on the wall-mounted TV.

I was free to go on my own recognizance.

On our way home, while Lilly sipped a conciliatory Whataburger chocolate shake, I turned to her in an effort to relieve the still-fresh pang of remorse.

"I'm so sorry, Lollipop," I said. "If I hadn't put that blender in the freezer sideways, none of this would've happened."

"It's okay, Mom," she said between sips. "It was just an accident."

As if Columbo found the smoking gun, as if Cagney & Lacey released me from lock-up, as if Ally McBeal rested my case, as if Judge Wapner rendered his final verdict, as if Kojak winked and said, "Who loves ya, baby?"—I was released from my self-imposed blame and declared myself not guilty.

SEASON 3 ◆ EPISODE 6

A MIDSUMMER NIGHT'S SCHEME

I was a teenager, and it was a typical summer's night. With our family vacation a whole month away and school not starting until September, I was dying for some excitement.

After cutting the grass and weeding the garden, supplemented with an hour of lying out in the sun coated in tanning oil, I was released by my parents to find whatever fun was available in our little town.

I made a telephone call to my best friend, Patti, like I always did, except for that boring summer when she had a boyfriend. I talked on my retro candlestick telephone, a sixteenth birthday present from my parents, while lying across the yellow bedspread on my mock-brass twin bed.

The first thing I did was confirm with Patti that neither of us had been invited to a party or had a date.

"Nope," was Patti's response. Just what I had suspected. Next, we needed to secure transportation for the evening. Patti's parents had taken out their brown Ford Fairmont station wagon for the evening, so I borrowed my father's enormous 1977 Chevy Blazer.

I picked up Patti at her house and—after we applied copious amounts of lip gloss and made sure our bangs looked just right—we headed out to cruise the town.

Our journey started with the usual drive by the local arcade,

Games 101, a hangout of sorts. Although Patti and I didn't give two shakes about *Asteroids* or *Ms. Pac-Man*, we knew the arcade was a veritable command center where information on teenage social events was collected and disseminated. Sometimes we scored big and received word of a bonfire in Bennett's woods or a party at the house of a classmate we all referred to as "Meatball," but on this particular night, the arcade was almost empty. Rather than driving around for hours all glossed up and trying to not look too desperate, we decided to scrape together a few of our girlfriends to pile into the Blazer and go check out the drive-in movie theater.

The only problem was, the Palace Gardens wasn't cheap. To avoid spending our hard-earned grass-cutting and ice-cream-scooping money on overpriced admission, we schemed how we might get into the drive-in on the cheap.

On previous occasions, we simply stuffed two of our friends, big hair and all, into the plywood dog crate my father had built into the back of the Blazer. It was nearly impossible to keep a straight face while driving by the ticket booth. But on this night, we hatched a more daring—and cheaper—plan. We would all sneak through the woods surrounding the Palace Gardens, and crawl through an opening in the fence to see the movie for free.

We met up at Patti's house, which was within walking distance of the drive-in, and the six of us made the attempt as a group. We had heard the rumors that the Palace Gardens management was cracking down on teens who refused to pay by lacing the fence with some kind of foul concoction made from watered down cow manure. We all knew nothing could ruin the chances of getting a boyfriend like stepping in manure, so we were all particularly cautious that night.

Using hand signals as if we were involved in some kind of special-ops raid on a drug lord's compound, we snuck through the woods, giggling and squealing, and breached the fence without incident. Or so we thought.

The nightly double feature included the new hit *Porky's*, but we weren't interested in the risqué scenes flashing on the jumbo outdoor screen. We headed straight for the large group of loitering teens near the concessions pavilion. Just before we reached the group, we realized one of our comrades had been hit.

"What's that smell?" Peggy whispered. Our noses quickly found the source of the pungent odor—Andrea's Jordache jeans had been tainted by the enemy's foul biological weapon. As teenage girls, we did not live by moral codes that compelled us to retrieve our wounded. We couldn't abandon our mission after such a successful secret adventure. Besides, Andrea was no diva. Refusing to spoil our fun, she headed home to change into some fresh jeans and meet up with us later, while the rest of us mingled among the cars under the stars on that balmy summer night.

The next night, and the nights after that, were filled with more of the same: Patti and I and our goofy girlfriends scanning the perimeters of our meager summer realm for whatever excitement could be had. Sometimes we found it at Games 101, at Buttermilk Falls, at Meatball's house, in Bennett's woods, at the Palace Gardens, and on very rare occasions, on a date. But many nights, we just drove around, glossed and teased, for hours—searching, planning, scheming.

Decades later, I would watch my own teens as they foraged for excitement on lazy summer nights. I smiled, realizing what they would understand someday, too—it's the scheming itself that is the most fun of all.

SEASON 3 ◆ EPISODE 7

THE ARMCHAIR OLYMPIAN

"I used to be a sprinter," Francis said, while he watched the Olympics with a bag of tortilla chips placed conveniently on his middle-aged gut.

Is he being serious? I thought.

"Are you being serious?" Anna asked from her seat on the floor.

"Oh, sure. Back in eighty-eight when I was in Aviation Officer Candidate School down in Pensacola, they recruited me to be a sprinter for field day."

I somehow kept my Diet Coke from shooting out of my nose and gave my skeptical daughter a knowing wink.

The Olympics had that effect on Francis. Despite his relatively sedentary middle-aged life, watching the Olympics compelled him to relive his youth, athleticism, and former waistline. I sympathized. We all like to tap into the time when we drove a used Chevette, didn't pay taxes, regularly ate cold pizza for breakfast, found no use for fiber supplements, and said things like, "Decent."

Ah, the good old days.

Thank goodness our children didn't know us back then. They made the perfect audience for this little ego trip down memory lane...or Fantasyland, as it were.

"Now you see," Francis bellowed from his BarcaLounger in our TV room during the men's quadruple sculls final, "In my crew days back at GW, we had to be in tip-top condition to be able to withstand the rigors of the sport." The kids looked on doubtfully.

I knew the truth, but I didn't want to burst Francis's bubble. Crew was something he did in college to enhance his image as the wrinkled-khaki-button-down-oxford-penny-loafer-preppy-frat-boy, in hopes it might score him a few decent chicks. He milked that gig until graduation, and then never set foot in a crew shell again.

But he analyzed the sport from his armchair as if he'd been an Olympic contender.

"See, that one there is the coxswain, who needs to be small and light. I was far too muscular for that position," he said between sips of beer.

I must admit I, too, have claimed former athletic prowess while watching the Olympics from the comfort of my well-worn spot on the couch.

"What you don't know about your mother is that I swam in college. Yup. We were Mid-American Conference Champions, so it was a pretty big deal."

I conveniently left out that I was one of only two walk-ons to try out for my college swim team. There were only two open spots, so the coach had to take us both. The other girl was way better than I was, but she quit after two weeks. That effectively made me the only walk-on, and the worst swimmer on the team by a mile.

The kids didn't need to know that part.

When the Summer Olympics came to an end, we had to once again face our middle-aged reality. But...the Winter Olympics were not far off.

Francis would most likely relive the winter he mastered the rope tow on the bunny slope during ski lessons in Maryland. And

I would revive the burgeoning talent I exhibited at the Mack Park ice skating rink during those snowy Pennsylvania winters so long ago.

We wouldn't mention that Francis hated ski lessons, and only agreed to go because his mother promised to buy him hot cocoa. And I would keep it my little secret that I never made a complete rotation around the skating rink without falling.

No need to spoil it for the kids.

SEASON 3 ◆ EPISODE 8

FEEL IT IN YOUR REAR

We universally accept that teenagers don't know much about life, so why do we allow them to propel two-ton combustion engines over concrete at high speeds? After many months of pumping the phantom brake and digging my fingernails into the armrests, I couldn't help but breathe a sigh of relief when Hayden got his driver's license.

After those long months of teaching Hayden to drive, I finally understood my own parents' plight.

It was the day of my sixteenth birthday, and I was twirling the barrel of my curling iron through my bangs. I heard my mother's voice calling from outside our brick ranch, "Sweet Pea! Come here, would ya?"

I groaned, rolled my eyes, and ignored.

"Honeybunch? C'mon, it'll only take a sec!" Maz continued, eventually appearing at my bedroom door. I sassed back at her, annoyed by what I saw as her rude interference with the crucial task of heightening my bangs.

Eventually, I succumbed to her pleas, but not without attitude. I appeared outside, slump-shouldered and eyes rolling, where the cause of the hubbub was revealed. On our lawn sat a pale blue 1974 Volkswagen Beetle tied up with an enormous yellow bow.

I offered no apology for my embarrassing behavior. Instead,

I screamed and ran to claim the gift, which I assumed I wholeheartedly deserved.

That day, my dad was going to help me deliver pizzas for a school fundraiser, and he thought it was the perfect opportunity for me to learn to use the Beetle's stick shift.

My hair properly coiffed, I jumped excitedly into the driver's seat and awaited Dad's instructions.

A gruff former college football player, Dad was not delicate. He operated on pure instinct, street smarts, and gut feelings. I, on the other hand, uncertain of any innate abilities, relied on conscious analysis. Dad didn't use maps, instructions, or cookbooks. I did. He used facial expression and volume to communicate more than words, while I spoke in great detail to explain my thoughts.

So, when it came time for me to learn how to drive a stick, we were not exactly compatible.

After several stalls, I eventually got the Beetle onto the road. I made every first-timer mistake—revving the engine, sputtering and stalling, rolling back after stopping on an incline, riding the clutch, and lurching. Each time, Dad bellowed, "Easy, easy! No, not now! There, now! Shift! The clutch, the clutch! Feel it in your rear!"

I couldn't process the words he was blasting in my ear, and I soon began to cry.

"Can't you feel it in your rear? That's how you know when to shift!" he shouted in frustration. I had no idea what he was talking about, and continued to grind, lurch, and stall.

I was able to hide my tears during the first few pizza deliveries, but when the Beetle stalled in the middle of Route 286, downhill from a barreling coal truck, my father had to yell even more to get the car started and us to safety.

I was soon a blubbering, red-eyed, snotty mess. It didn't help my delivery patter at the next stop.

"Hello—*sniff*—ma'am, I—I—I believe—*snort*—you ordered

two—*hiccup*—pepperoni pizzas?" I managed to stammer out, rubbing my nose on my sleeve between my halting words.

"Oh, Sweetie, sure!" said the lady who answered the door. "Would you like to come inside and sit a while?"

I somehow managed to finish the deliveries without anyone calling child protective services but was devastated at my failure to understand my father's instructions. Later, I took the Beetle out alone on the road in front of our house. Even though I still didn't feel anything in my rear, I was surprised at how quickly I taught myself to shift successfully through the gear pattern.

Decades later, I realized being a passenger in a car being driven by your own teenager can be a real pain in the butt. Maybe that's what Dad was talking about.

SEASON 3 ◆ EPISODE 9

THE CHAINS OF LOVE

Francis was deeply in love with someone. Someone with a great personality. Someone who made him feel like a real man. Someone with a really nice tush.

That someone was himself.

I was envious of his self-respect and confidence. I'd been trying my entire life to be satisfied with myself, but the best I could muster was the fleeting thought, *I'm not so bad for a housewife*.

By contrast, Francis's ego was ironclad, and completely undiminished by hereditary balding, an ample spare tire, and no mechanical skills. He couldn't even walk by a mirror or other reflective object without admiring his image. Every time he caught a glimpse of himself, he stretched his neck out a bit, sucked in his gut, and twisted to sneak a peek at his backside. It seemed to reassure him, *Yup, I'm as good-looking as I think I am*.

Francis's self-admiration reached new heights thanks to his volunteer job with our kids' high school football team. On Friday nights, he would slip into his Blue Devils jersey, double-knotting his sneakers and giving himself a wink in the mirror before heading to the stadium.

At the ticket booth, he would proudly say loud enough for everyone in line to hear, "I'm on the entry list—chain gang." As a sacred volunteer, he sauntered through the gate without paying, as if he were Snoop Dogg being ushered through the velvet ropes at Studio 54.

He and the other chain gang dads gathered near concessions for their weekly pregame huddle. After handshakes and back slaps, they haggled over team stats and joked loudly, glancing around to see who was watching.

Just before kickoff, Francis slipped into the back door of the concession booth to obtain the first of three cheeseburgers he would consume throughout the course of the night. Unfortunately, the volunteer coordinator had offered the chain gang dads free food, and Francis took full advantage, deeming it absolutely necessary for sustenance.

Cheeseburger No. 1 went down in four chomps, and Francis disposed of the wrapper in one manly whip at the trash cans before marching purposefully across the lighted field to take his coveted position on the chains. As he approached the opposing team's side, he relished his elevated status. Not everyone could walk onto the field minutes before kick-off, but he could because he was chosen to be in the inner circle of football volunteers. Not just any volunteer, but the kind that entered for free, walked on the field, and ate anything he wanted. Francis had reached the top echelon, the pinnacle, the upper crust of the football volunteer hierarchy, and he knew it.

After withstanding the grueling rigors of holding a pole for two whole fifteen-minute football game quarters, Francis made a shamelessly public display of running back across the field at half time in search of more refreshments. He chugged a can of soda as if he'd just finished an Iron Man competition in Death Valley and tossed the can with a masculine belch. Cheeseburger No. 2 was consumed with a serious demeanor. There was still work to be done.

Thankfully, the six-hundred-calorie burger gave Francis the strength he needed to endure holding a pole for the last half of the game. When the final whistle was blown, and the game was called, Francis paraded his weary body back across the field one last time, waving and winking on the way as if he were an integral member of the coaching staff.

Despite his exhaustion, he moved swiftly because he knew he must get to the concession before closing time. Cheeseburger No. 3 in hand, he took his place on the track to allow exiting spectators to get a good look at the illustrious chain gang.

Back at home, Francis carefully hung his jersey back in the closet to await the next game and readied himself for bed. Another glance in the mirror confirmed what he already knew— he was everything he ever wanted, and more.

SEASON 3 ◆ EPISODE 10

TEAM MOM SURVIVAL TIPS

It was my favorite time of year—high school football season—and even though I knew volunteer work could be a real hassle, I just wanted to be *a part of it all*.

I casually told Hayden's football coach I would "help out," which I thought meant I had agreed to send out a few emails, sell t-shirts, or bake cupcakes for the team dinners. However, I had just unknowingly leaped into a vast, dark chasm of unknown perils.

At some point, the coach began referring to me as "Team Mom." Initially, I was flattered, because the new title seemed so loving, so nurturing. I envisioned the players giving me side hugs as I bandaged their boo-boos and offered them freshly baked cookies.

I soon discovered accepting the Team Mom title meant I was also expected to coordinate volunteers, type up and copy programs, raise thousands of dollars, plan the team banquet, throw a tailgate fundraiser, research and analyze complicated state regulations regarding 501(c)(3) nonprofit status, and split the atom.

Soon, I was forced to say goodbye to the things I once held dear—a clean house, home-cooked meals, a good night's sleep, free time, sanity. I had unwittingly accepted hazardous duty without pay, and I had to learn to survive.

I also learned I had to watch out for The Haters. Apparently, becoming Team Mom had given me instant mortal enemies. The reasons were complicated, but those two innocent-sounding words, when placed together and assigned to a middle-aged housewife, incited extreme resentment, territorial hostilities, power struggles, bitter rivalries, and threats of violence.

When the booster club president approached me in an aggressive manner after the game and said, "So, who's in charge here, YOU or ME?" I found out what she really meant was, "Listen, who the *bleep* do you think you are coming along with your smiley face and your Bermuda shorts, trying to steal my limelight? Get this straight: I like getting my ego stroked, and you are cramping my style. So back off."

Also, there was one particular football parent who seemed to have it out for me. In addition to throwing killer glares and snide remarks my way as often as possible, she also cornered me during the tailgate fundraiser to accuse me of "messing up" the hot dog pricing. I was initially confused, until I realized what she really meant was, "Make no mistake about it, due to insecurities rooted in childhood, I have made it my goal to turn all the other moms against you because it makes me feel powerful, and I thrive on drama."

Thankfully, I did not lose control of my bowels. Instead I smiled, pleaded ignorance, and carried on as if nothing had happened. Although I did make a mental note to start packing pepper spray.

As Team Mom, I became the inbox for every imaginable parent grievance about practice time, meeting time, position assignments, equipment distribution, fundraising, and penalty calls. I had no real authority to change anything, but the parents knew that. They weren't asking for change. They were really saying, "We have no intention of complaining directly to the coach, because it might negatively impact our sons' playing time. So, when we feel like launching into a bitter rant, we expect you to take it like one of those inflatable clown punching bags."

Other than publicizing the coach's cell phone number, the only thing I could do was learn how to *look* like a concerned listener, while singing the refrain from "I Will Survive" repeatedly in my head.

I learned valuable lessons from the experience: how to sell snow cones and price hotdogs, how to avoid Mean Lady and Hostile Mom in the parking lot, and how to appear sympathetic to Whiny Parent's harangue about the odor of her son's cleats, without taking in a single word. Also, I knew all of it, no matter how difficult or painful, had helped the team. I knew my son and the other players had made lasting memories, and I had been part of it all.

And I learned the most important Team Mom lesson: Convince some other sucker to do the job next year.

SEASON 3 ◆ EPISODE 11

A CHRISTMAS CAROL, REDUX

Thanksgiving was over.

For some reason, my sports watch alarm went off at midnight, waking me from a strange dream. In the nightmare, I had been unable to run from a creature molded from leftover stuffing and mashed potatoes with gravy dripping from its outstretched arms, due to the weight of my own enormous thighs.

I started to drift off again, when a form suddenly appeared at the foot of my bed. She wore a floor-length, polyester, red-and-green-plaid skirt, a white ruffled blouse with a huge tab collar, a crocheted vest, and a Christmas tree pin.

"Hi, like, I'm the Ghost of Christmas Past, and I'm here to take you on, like, a pretty decent trip back to the seventies," the apparition said while twirling a segment of her long hair. No sooner did I grasp the ghost's braided macramé belt than we were whisked on metal roller skates to the home of my youth.

It was two weeks before Christmas 1974, and Maz was preparing her shopping list while Tray and I decorated the Christmas tree with silver tinsel, careful not to rest the tiny plastic strips on the blazing hot bubble lights.

Maz's list included the names of our little family, along with aunts, uncles, cousins, and grandparents. She had saved enough in her Christmas account to buy fruitcake, tea towels, Avon perfume, Barbies, Tonka trucks, and decorative tins of ribbon candies.

Although Tray and I loved to go downtown to see shops decorated with lights and mechanical elves, that night we begged to stay home so we would not miss the new Rankin Bass special, *The Year Without a Santa Claus*, which our console television might pick up if the antenna was turned just right.

Maz agreed to put off shopping one more day. Instead, she wrote out her twelve Christmas cards and served us cocoa in Santa mugs with cookies, which we were disappointed to find contained prunes, raisins, molasses, mincemeat, anise, or some other objectionable ingredient. Nevertheless, we lay contentedly on the green shag rug listening to a Burl Ives record, gazing up at our tree and its Styrofoam egg-carton star.

I reached out toward this vision of my youth, but was wrenched from my trance when a bubble light scorched my arm. "Ouch!" I exclaimed, and was abruptly dumped back into my own bed, surrounded by nothing but the dark night and a faint tapping sound.

I soon found the source of the tapping. Seated on the end of the bed, her thumbs poking away at an iPhone, was the second apparition. She glanced at me and said, "Hey, how's it going? I'm the Ghost of Christmas Present, but hold on a sec, I have to answer this."

Finally, the specter finished texting and proclaimed, "Alrighty, touch my yoga pants and let's do this thing, because I've got carpool duty in a couple hours." I grabbed her spandex waistband and was transported to scenes of unimaginable Christmas chaos.

First, we saw the three-page Christmas list I'd made right after Halloween, which included gifts for the school lunch ladies, Anna's ukulele instructor, the seven neighbors we like, and the three we don't but can't leave off the list for fear of inciting neighborhood conflict.

Next, we joined a stampede of Black Friday shoppers, all poised to pepper spray each other over the last Play Station game console at Walmart. Then the Spirit took me to Starbucks, where we paid five dollars for a mocha peppermint chai tea and three hundred dollars for gift cards for the kids' teachers. Then we dashed home to type, print, and mail out 150 copies of the annual family Christmas letter, replete with exaggerated superlatives about the kids and the daily activities of our dog.

Then we ate, and ate, and ate. Everything from gallons of hot dip to platters of cookies packed with peanut butter chips, candy chunks, marshmallows, and M&Ms. We washed it all down with cartons of eggnog which, according to the sell-by date, would still be potable come Valentine's Day.

Finally, the Ghost of Christmas Present dropped me in front of our HDTV virtual fireplace glowing beside our artificial tree with its economical LED lights. Exhausted and embarrassed by the modern-day holiday delirium, I pleaded, "Have mercy, Spirit! Haunt me no more!"

Just then, a figure approached from the shadows, cloaked in a black hooded garment. "Are you the Ghost of Christmases Yet to Come?!" I yelped in fear. The apparition nodded silently and handed me a small high-tech device. With a swipe, I activated a life-sized holographic Christmas tree. A second click started microwaving a frozen Tofurky dinner with vegan trimmings. In mere nanoseconds, I sent warmly personalized holiday video messages to friends of friends of friends on Facebook.

But then, the Spirit pointed a long finger at the futuristic device. On the screen appeared countless images of pale people sitting alone in the dark, without family and friends, without fresh pine and twinkle lights, without hot cocoa and old movies, without music and laughter. They sat alone, clicking buttons on Christmas.

"No, Spirit!" I cried, repeating over and over, "I promise I will heed these lessons and honor Christmas in my heart!"

As if it had all been a dream, I awoke in my own bed and rushed excitedly down the stairs, shouting to my daughter, "Turn off that virtual fireplace this minute, Lillian Molinari!"

"Anna!" I bellowed, "Preheat the oven! We have cookies to bake!"

"Come and witness this glorious morning, young man!" I called up to Hayden, who was still slumbering soundly.

To Francis I demanded, "Off with you, my good man, to the Winn-Dixie for the fattest turkey in the freezer case!"

I ripped up my three-page shopping list. I tied a big red bow on the dog's collar. I rifled through the pantry for cocoa and mini marshmallows. I blasted my favorite Sinatra holiday CD and danced silly circles around our kitchen.

God bless us, every one, I thought with a full heart. Bless us, every one—not virtually, but truly.

SEASON 3 ◆ EPISODE 12

WORKING OUT A TIME
TO WORK OUT

Did this thing shrink? I wondered, while stuffing the relevant bits and pieces into my sports bra. I had resolved to drop a few excess pounds after the holidays, and putting on workout clothes was half the battle.

"Now I *have* to exercise today," I mumbled before trudging to the kitchen for coffee.

After driving the kids to school in our dirty white minivan, I headed home, fully intending to jog directly to the base gym and lift weights. Pulling into my driveway, I noticed the messy interior of the van and decided I had to vacuum the van before my run.

There's something about Shop-Vacs, leaf blowers, and power washers. Once I get the tool going, I can't seem to put the thing down. It's exhilarating to cleanse one's life of debris and clutter, and I never want that feeling to end.

Two hours later, I had not only vacuumed the van, I had also sucked the cobwebs out of the garage, the sand off the screened porch, the dog hair off the living room floor, the peanuts from under the couch cushions, and the crumbs out of the utensil drawers.

I breathed a huge sigh of cleansed relief, and then noticed the time. "Criminy!" I blurted, "I need to get on that jog!" I decided to save the weight lifting for the following day, and just get the run in. *But before I go, I thought, I'd better hit the bathroom.*

My middle-aged bladder no longer cooperates. I was always one of those girls who could hold it forever like some kind of Arabian camel. But once I hit age forty, my bladder got fed up and took my urethra hostage. Essentially, when the urge strikes, I'd better find the bathroom pronto, or my bladder will open the release valve on my own little Hoover Dam.

While doing my business, I noticed an interesting article on space exploration in the latest *National Geographic*.

Amidst a resounding flush, I emerged from the bathroom with an empty bladder and a brain full of newfound information on space exploration, scatology, airborne microbes, and Ecuadorian parakeets.

"Fascinating," I muttered while tying up the string on my workout pants.

It was on the early side of lunchtime according to the clock. I couldn't go on a run with an empty stomach, of course. Ever a multitasker, I ate lunch at the computer while checking emails.

Computers can be evil. Just like I can't just buy one thing at Target, I find it nearly impossible to just "check email." Somehow, tabs get opened, links get clicked, and next thing you know, I've told someone what I ate for lunch on Facebook, bid on a set of vintage Pyrex nesting bowls on eBay, and watched three YouTube videos of babies laughing.

Suddenly my watch alarm beeped, signaling it was time to get back in the minivan to pick up the kids from school. "Well, darn it," I huffed, "I guess I'll have to power walk later this afternoon."

A couple of hours later, I was ready for that walk, but first decided I'd better fluff and fold the laundry real quick so Francis's uniforms wouldn't wrinkle. Since folding laundry is about as fun as watching paint dry, I flipped on the TV.

I must say, those shows about hoarders are riveting. Like a

train wreck, they're awful and tragic, but you can't stop watching.

An hour later, I *had* to defrost the chicken; I *had* to take Lilly to her tennis lesson; I *had* to load the dishwasher; I *had* to scratch the dog's belly; I *had* to watch that new episode of *Modern Family*.

At 10:00 p.m., Francis woke me on the couch to lead me to bed. My workout clothes were quite cozy, so in a *Flashdance*-inspired move, I took off my sports bra and climbed right into bed.

My workout clothes will already be on when I wake up in the morning, I thought to myself before dropping off to sleep, so *I'll have to exercise tomorrow, for sure.*

SEASON 3 ◆ EPISODE 13

ONE OF THOSE DAYS

I always believed I'd be able to manage our family life without compromising my standards. Apparently, I was wrong, because there I was crying like a baby while careening down the expressway in my dingy minivan. Wearing my standard black workout pants, ratty tennis shoes, and a fleece jacket adorned with dog hair, I struggled to see through my tears and the bug guts still on the windshield from our spring break trip. All three kids sat in their seats, unfazed. They'd seen this kind of crazed display before.

It had been one of those days. This time, the breaking point occurred during an after-school conference with Hayden's English teacher. News of our son's academic transgressions, coupled with the normal events of everyday life—work deadlines, dirty laundry, the price of gas, dust bunnies, hormones—was just enough to bring me to the brink.

And I used to be so sure of myself....

One dreary winter before Lilly was born, Francis and I traveled to Boston to visit his old college roommate who, like Francis, was married with kids, a job, and a mortgage. They were a few years ahead of our life schedule, so visiting them was like looking into our future.

While our husbands snuck off to drink beer somewhere, I

hung out with the other wife as she went about her day as a stay-at-home mom to three kids.

Riding in her dingy minivan to school, I felt a subtle twinge of anxiety. My counterpart was somewhat tensely gripping the wheel, wearing her husband's jacket, workout pants marred with a blob of dried schmutz, slippers, and a pair of broken sunglasses that sat crooked on her face. The floor of the van was strewn with debris—discarded kids' meal toys, juice boxes, crumpled wrappers, and tidbits of food.

As she chatted about leaving her career as an attorney to raise the kids, my mind wandered. *What is that stuff on her pants? Can't she scrape it off with her thumbnail? With those glasses cocked sideways, she looks like she might suddenly run us all off a cliff. At least if we are stranded in a ravine, we could survive a few days on the old french fries and Skittles under the seats.*

Back at her house, she washed out two dirty cups, served us some coffee and slumped into a scratched kitchen chair with the newspaper. I could tell that skimming the newspaper over coffee each day was her one indulgence and depriving her of this little break from her chaotic routine might just sever her precarious hold on sanity.

I puttered to allow her time to read.

"Hey, listen to this," she suddenly commanded. "A man filed a missing persons report because his wife and mother of their children disappeared last week. Don't you know, they found her, happily living in a newly rented apartment. Apparently, she loved her family dearly but desperately needed a break, so she ran away."

My crazed hostess lifted her head from her paper and stared out the window for a few seconds before mumbling, "She...just...ran away."

"I need to go freshen up a bit," I lied, and hid in the bathroom in hopes she would find solace and not a loaded weapon.

On the plane ride home, I thought of how the woman seemed to be hanging on by a thread and told myself I would *never* lead such a cluttered, disorganized, chaotic life.

And yet, fourteen years later, there I was in my own dingy minivan, wearing my own schmutzy pants, crying my eyes out over my own chaotic life. As I said, the kids had seen it all before. They knew I'd soon be back to "normal," which for me was a mental state that vacillated between Supermom and somewhat unstable.

But, I did not drive our minivan off a cliff or run away to find a new life for myself. No, much like the old college roommate's wife in Boston, I maintained my grip on that invisible thread from which we moms hang and did what I needed to do to survive the chaos.

On that particular afternoon, it only took a good cry, an entire can of Pringles, and two episodes of *Dance Moms* for me to make a full recovery. Ironically, I was proud of myself and mothers everywhere, who, despite it all, continue to muster the strength to face "one of those days."

SEASON 3 ◆ EPISODE 14

BRACING FOR BANKRUPTCY

I was sitting in the orthodontist's waiting room, again, all finished organizing the items in my purse, looking for something else to keep me occupied until Anna's monthly adjustments were complete. I'd done it all: balanced my checkbook, applied concealer to the dark circles under my eyes, watched *Toy Story*, torn recipes out of magazines. I'd even discovered an old cough drop in the bottom of my purse, picked off the lint, and eaten it.

With three kids in braces, it seemed like I'd spent half my life in the orthodontist's waiting room, and unfortunately, half our combined income too.

I'd never thought my kids' teeth looked all that crooked in the first place, but somehow they *all* needed full orthodontic treatment including preparatory extractions, palate expanders, bands, brackets, adjustments, headgear, and retainers.

My intuition whispered this was nothing more than a widespread conspiracy between our dentist, oral surgeon, orthodontist, and insurance company to swindle me out of as much money as possible. They knew all they had to do was use big words, show me some murky x-rays, and put the fear of God in me that my kids' mouths would soon become veritable train wrecks of snaggleteeth. They knew I would cave, and that's exactly what I had done.

Sitting in the same gaudy upholstered waiting room chair I'd sat in a thousand times, I glanced up at the animated movie that was hypnotizing patients' younger siblings into compliance.

The image of *Snow White* brought to mind memories of my own childhood, when the general attitude toward additional hardware such as orthodontics, glasses, orthopedic shoes, and back braces was that they were instant fodder for bullying and should be avoided if at all possible. I recalled the unfortunate experience of having braces when I was in the fifth grade. My orthodontist certainly didn't have to use his powers of persuasion to convince my parents to pay. On the contrary, my parents were begging on bended knee, "Please, for the love of God, do something about her teeth!" which were spread so far apart, Tray had begun referring to me as "The Rake."

I harrumphed out loud, remembering that my braces were not trendy modern appliances with inconspicuously glued brackets, colorful bands, and thin sparkling wire. No. Every tooth in my eleven-year-old head was cemented with gun-metal grey steel bands welded with cumbersome brackets connected by thick wire. Rather than enhancing my appearance, I went from looking like "The Rake" to resembling Jaws from 007's *The Spy Who Loved Me.*

And of course, how could I forget the dreaded headgear? "Here, pick one," the orthodontist had offered me, pointing to a big bin of colorful neck straps to go with my new hardware. I chose the stylish faux denim option, a wholly inadequate consolation prize for the utter humiliation of wearing the slobber-producing device.

I heaved a sigh and chuckled inwardly at the awkward memories of those bygone braces.

With twenty minutes of waiting left to go and nothing to do but pick stuff out from under my fingernails, I tried to ignore the internal cynic who thought of all the money being automatically withdrawn from our dwindling checking account in the name of orthodontic perfection and middle-school fashion. Instead, I comforted myself with the knowledge that at least my purse had never been more organized.

SEASON 3 ◆ EPISODE 15

THE FAMILY MEETING

"**C**'mon guys!" I bellowed from the kitchen, "You're late!" One by one, they appeared at our table, each carrying a heavy attitude.

Francis had always thought my family meetings were pure nonsense. All this nicey-nicey talking was a complete waste of his Sunday leisure time. When he grew up, you did what your parents told you to do, or you'd be wearing five faster than you could say "child protective services."

However, Francis had left me in charge of the household on so many occasions during our marriage while he was deployed or traveling for his military job, he had decided it was best to go along with my parenting schemes, harebrained or not.

I'd been holding semi-annual family meetings since the kids were too young to read my typed agendas, and I believed these forced family events were necessary to maintain order and my sanity. I suppose I was afraid we'd turn our kids into axe murders, heroin junkies, or worst of all, adults with low self-esteem.

So I believed we could achieve total cooperation from our children simply by gathering them up and nicely telling them what we wanted them to do.

Lilly and Anna arrived in a sock-sliding race for the best seat, the elder sister grabbing the prime spot.

The last to arrive, thudding down the stairs, was Hayden,

who would have preferred a week-long insurance seminar to a conversation with family during which feelings might be discussed.

With everyone seated, I played upon their worst fears.

"Okay, everyone, let's hold hands and say what we love about each other."

I allowed a few seconds of uncomfortable silence, and just when I thought mutiny was imminent I blurted, "Gotcha!" My comedic genius softened them up a bit, exactly what I needed for my parental brainwashing plan to take hold. Clearing my throat, I began.

"School starts tomorrow, and we want you to manage your time properly so everything runs smoothly. We'll get up each morning promptly at six, and we expect..." I went on and on about bedtimes, homework, chores, allowance, privileges, personal hygiene, and manners.

About forty minutes into the lecture, I knew I was losing them, an eventuality for which I was prepared.

"In conclusion, to help you manage your time, we got you each a little gift."

The girls squealed with delight when I revealed three super-cool new sports watches, with digital displays, dual alarms with five-minute back up, ten-lap memory chrono, and water resistance to 100 meters—whatever all that means.

I sat back, smug with satisfaction. *Rules will be followed. Order is restored. No punishments necessary. And I look like Mother Teresa. My plan is complete.*

"Uh, just so you know, I'm not wearing this thing," Hayden interjected.

"Listen Honey, you're almost a man now—you really should learn how to use a watch."

"I'm not putting this stupid hunk of plastic on my wrist when there are clocks everywhere."

I can't be sure, but I believe smoke started emanating from my ears.

It may have been Hayden's utter lack of appreciation, his complete disregard for authority, my unrealistic desire for total obedience, or that my underwear was riding up that afternoon, but I was seeing red.

"Listen to me, young man," I said through gritted teeth, "you WILL wear that watch, you understand me?"

"NO."

The next twenty minutes were a bit foggy, but I clearly recall Francis storming off down the street and Hayden throwing the watch at the wall while screaming a particular expletive he'd previously not uttered in our presence. Then I vaguely remember flying upstairs without touching the ground and lifting Hayden's door off the hinges with superhuman strength.

Cooling off in our garage, I felt an immediate sense of regret. *The boy IS seventeen—he probably sees that watch as a shackle, keeping him under our control. I need to let him make his own choice.*

I walked into the house, just as Hayden was coming out to find me. Our eyes met, communicating our mutual regret without words.

"Where'd that watch go, Mom? If you want, I'll give it a try."

"I'll help you find it, Honey....But I was thinking, you could just carry it in your pocket if you don't want to wear it around your wrist. Or, you don't have to wear it at all." We smiled at each other, realizing how silly we'd been.

Just as I found the watch in the corner, Francis arrived home, refreshed from a nice afternoon walk, and asked, "So...what's for dinner?"

SEASON 3 ◆ EPISODE 16

365 DAYS AND COUNTING

"You think you got it bad now," other moms cautioned me one afternoon when Hayden, Anna, and Lilly were small, "just wait till they're teenagers."

Like the weird sisters of *Macbeth*, they gave each other knowing glances and chuckled as they watched me nearly amputate a foot trying get my screaming toddler's stroller onto the escalator at the mall.

I walked away thinking those moms were just old and bitter. I summarily dismissed their annoying prophecies. I firmly believed whatever stage of parenting I was experiencing was the worst one, and no one was going to convince me otherwise.

Then when Hayden turned seventeen, it occurred to me that only one year of his childhood remained. I wasn't sure if I should celebrate or burst into tears.

The first time I held my son in my arms, I felt an awesome sense of love and purpose. In an instant, my own needs shifted from my top priority to a distant second, and I couldn't have been happier about it. Like any mama bear, squirrel, or flamingo, focus on my own survival automatically switched to the endurance of my offspring.

Although it is initially a joy to put our children's needs ahead of our own, over time the task of parenting gets bothersome, frustrating, and frankly, downright terrifying. Nowhere would this fact of life become clearer than when Hayden became a teenager.

I hated to admit it, but those cackling witches at the mall were right as rain.

When Hayden turned thirteen, his head didn't spin, his eyes didn't roll, and foul expletives didn't burst forth from his mouth. No, he was the same kid he'd always been. When he turned fourteen we saw subtle changes—his first shave, a deepening voice, reluctance to accept affection.

How cute, we thought.

We drifted contentedly into our son's teen years, comfortably secure that *our* teenager would *never* be a problem, because we were *good* parents and had raised him *right*.

But soon after the candles on our son's Rubik's Cube-shaped fifteenth birthday cake were extinguished, a new period of parenting ensued, which might best be described as "Armageddon."

Suddenly, the bathroom door was permanently locked. Hayden stopped making eye contact. A foul smell hung like a green fog in his bedroom. He snickered secretly into the phone behind his barricaded bedroom door. When we managed to catch sight of him in the flesh, he was always asleep.

In what seemed like an instant, the sweet boy we had known all those years turned into a smelly, undisciplined stranger who, apparently, hated our guts.

At night we lay in bed, our minds racing with anger, frustration, guilt, and panicked thoughts of our son's future. Desperate, we listened to other parents of teens, and found out the hell we were experiencing was actually quite common.

Apparently, just as new hairs sprout from a teen's body, a budding new attitude develops in the teen brain. The once dependent, reverent child suddenly thinks:

There's nothing I don't already know. I will now run my own life. I find you, my parents, totally embarrassing and reserve the right to roll my eyes in pure disgust whenever I see fit. I will, however, continue to associate with you so you can buy me a car, electronics, clothing of my choice, pizza for me and my friends, and a place to sleep until two in the afternoon. Oh, and don't forget to save upwards of one hundred thousand dollars to send me off to college so I can reenact Animal House *at your expense.*

When I realized there was only one year left before Hayden would be off to college, you'd think I would have chilled champagne and made plans to fumigate his room. But ironically, I was melancholy and knew I was at risk of becoming one of the witches, warning young moms to appreciate the days when their biggest problem was getting the stroller onto the escalator at the mall.

SEASON FOUR

IN IT TO WIN IT

SEASON 4 ◆ EPISODE 1

THE OLD MAN
AND THE DEGREE

About an hour into the trip, I blew a royal gasket.

"If you think for one cotton-picking minute that I'm just here to play chauffeur while you visit these colleges, you'd better think again!" I blared at Hayden from the driver's seat as our car chugged down the Massachusetts Turnpike.

I knew our weekend trip to visit two colleges in Upstate New York was one of those ephemeral opportunities for me to bond with Hayden, and I had planned to make the best of it.

Ever well intentioned, I peppered Hayden with friendly questions about his interests, friends, and school, in hopes that one of my probes would ignite an in-depth mother-son conversation to pass the time. However, my inquiries were met with typical resistance, eliciting only grunts, one-word answers, and the dreaded eye roll.

I just couldn't take it anymore, and I snapped.

During my cathartic rant, I explained to Hayden that the college trip was an important step in his becoming an independent person, a responsible adult, a man. I told him refusing to converse with his mother who was facilitating and financing the trip was not only rude, it was *immature*.

He hated that word, so I strategically ended with it, and then fell silent.

A few miles later, Hayden asked me a question. Not "Are we there yet?" or "When are you going to buy me dinner?" but a well-planned dialogue starter. We conversed for a few fleeting minutes before he fell sound asleep.

Three hours later, he awoke to our GPS announcing, "You have arrived at your destination."

I quelled the awkwardness of sharing a hotel room with then eighteen-year-old Hayden by ordering pizza and resisting the urge to remind him to brush his teeth. Soon after his three-hour car nap, he sprawled on his bed in sweatpants and headphones and dropped off to sleep for the night.

Knowing the days of seeing my children sleep would soon be over, I lingered a minute or two before turning out the light, watching his chest heave and his eyelids twitch.

In the morning, we found ourselves following a bubbly backward-walking female tour guide along angled walkways, between ivy-covered academic buildings and through student unions. The campus looked beautiful in the autumnal morning light, but I was watching Hayden for hints of reaction. I knew if I asked him what he thought of the school, he'd give me the same half-grunted response every time: "M'good."

Despite my warning, Hayden wolfed down a meatball sub for lunch in the car on our way to the next college. Once in the lobby of the admissions building, without saying, "I told you so," I showed him to the restroom where he could blot the red sauce stains off his tie.

After the tour, we had a scheduled meeting with a professor, to discuss the requirements of the computer science degree. The professor's bio indicated that he had done cutting-edge research on the science behind modern social media networks, so we were surprised to be met by a sweet old gentleman with a Russian accent, white hair, and a mild palsy in his left hand.

The professor spoke softly across his cluttered desk,

whispering sage advice to Hayden about his college years.

"You must use this time in your life," he paused to emit an almost imperceptible gasp, before continuing, "...to become a man."

Still splotched with signs of lunch, Hayden listened intently, unable to hide his utter admiration for this master of computer science. With eager eyes, he asked questions about programming languages, algorithms, and data structures. I sat, dumbfounded, while the old professor and my son built a delightful rapport. Forty-five minutes later, they exchanged wide grins and sincere handshakes, promising to keep in touch.

On the ride home, while Hayden slept soundly in the seat beside me, I thought about the old professor's "you're a man now" advice. Francis and I had told him the same thing so many times. *Why doesn't he listen to us?*

An exit or two later, I recollected that during the meeting with the old professor, I saw Hayden successfully communicate his intentions, ask mature questions, and show genuine respect like an intelligent adult.

I glanced over at my splotched, grunting, stubborn young man and realized he had been listening all along.

SEASON 4 ◆ EPISODE 2

MY HIPS DON'T SWING THAT WAY, BUT MY BELLY DOES

It wasn't easy showing up at the base gym the week after Christmas, after such a long and unexplained hiatus. I knew my presence would be perceived as a half-hearted attempt at a New Year's resolution, most likely to fizzle before the first week of February. I gave myself a little pep talk in the parking lot.

Just parade in there like you own the place. For all they know, you've been running marathons and playing rugby for the past year.

Yeah, what do they know? I responded to my own pep talk.

Approaching the front desk, I flashed my military ID, hoping no one would see me before I darted off to Zumba class.

"Is that you, Mrs. Molinari?" Nick, one of the gym staff called from behind the desk. His intonation and use of "Mrs." notified everyone within earshot that some old lady who hasn't been to the gym in a long time finally showed up. I waved sheepishly and slunk off to class.

Expecting to see the room packed with twenty-something hard bodies that would send me into a tailspin of self-loathing, I was relieved to find a comforting mix of people, all with their share of bodily imperfections and jiggly bits. After placing my keys and water bottle in the corner of the cramped exercise room, I found a spot where I could remain anonymous.

Our instructor resembled a middle-aged mom like me, and she did not have a figure that screamed, "I'm obsessed with fitness." She hit a button on the sound system and gave us a short introduction. I didn't bother listening. *It's just dancing...how difficult could it be?*

Then I remembered that Francis and I have been botching the Electric Slide at every military ball, holiday party, and wedding reception since our own in 1993. Same goes for the Cha Cha Slide, the Macarena, and the Cupid Shuffle. Call us choreographically challenged, we couldn't Whip, Nae Nae, or Stanky Leg if our lives depended on it.

Our instructor put on some catchy Latin music, and I was kick-ball-changing, single-single-doubling, and body rolling my way around the room as if I had been doing it all my life.

After thirty minutes, the mild-mannered instructor announced that our "warm up" was finished. The *real* Zumba class was about to begin, and the *real* instructor was on her way.

What?

I had only a moment to glug some water from my bottle, when in walked a woman garbed in skin-tight black spandex with Tina Turner's spiky hair, Beyoncé's muscular thighs, Pamela Anderson's generous bust, and Charo's rolling rrrrr's.

Suddenly, driving African beats blared from the sound system and, using only facial expressions and minimal hand motions, she ordered us to rhythmically gyrate and flail our arms while in a semi-squat position.

A few minutes later we moved on to reggaetón, whatever that is, and were commanded to stick out our rear ends and rotate our hips in complete circles from right to left while pumping our hands out in front of us. For some unknown reason, I was able to rotate my hips counter clockwise, but as soon as we were asked to go in the opposite direction, I was unable to maintain the fluidity of my hips and could only jerk from side to side.

I thought perhaps this was due to the magnetism of the earth's poles. And perhaps, like the water in toilet bowls, I can only swirl one way in the Northern Hemisphere and would have to go south of the equator to rotate my hips in the other direction.

Halfway through the class, my thighs were shaking, so I was relieved that we were moving on to salsa, something I'd at least heard of before and had enjoyed with chips.

Though everyone else seemed to have the basic salsa steps down pat, I was so confused I just started marching in place. I tried to mimic our limber instructor as she swiveled back and forth across the room, but all I could muster were a few awkward hops, several misplaced kick-ball-changes, inappropriate pelvic thrusts, and my own freestyle version of the pony.

We moved on to merengue, which for me, was more of a lesson in how to sprain one's ankle. I prayed it would all be over soon.

Somewhere between the Brazilian samba and the Columbian cumbia, our instructor started jumping three feet into the air. Like lemmings, we followed. Happy to have a dance move I could finally understand, I leapt like a gazelle. But then I remembered— I'm almost fifty years old and have given birth to three large babies. My innards are not where they used to be and might drop out onto the floor at any moment.

Thankfully, the jumping routine ended before my uterus broke loose, and we moved on to our final dance—a Bollywood belly dance. At first, it seemed our leader was merely putting us through a cruel endurance test when she demanded that we get into a deep plié squat while holding our arms out in ninety-degree angles like King Tut. Just as my quads were about to snap, she began to twist and turn her torso back and forth, rising like a cobra from a basket.

Despite my alarming heart rate, I only sported a small sweat mustache when the forty-five-minute class ended. Rather than exercise more, I hopped in the locker room sauna to wake my hibernating glands. Then I made the fatal mistake of following up the sauna with a scalding hot shower, opening veritable flood gates of profuse sweat that didn't ease up until mid-afternoon.

I left the gym feeling exhausted and humiliated but determined to keep my fitness goals. While it was obvious my northern European genes had rendered me unable to perform the sexy writhing Zumba moves correctly, at least I could be proud that, somehow, my belly kept perfect time to the beat.

SEASON 4 ◆ EPISODE 3

LADY SURGERY

It was Super Bowl Sunday, and while our friends were getting ready to gorge on hot chicken wings, icy cold beers, creamy dips, and spicy chili slathered in onions and cheese, I was guzzling sixty-four ounces of a pharmaceutical concoction to prepare for surgery.

Surgery. The day after the Super Bowl. *Lucky me.*

Preoperative bowel cleansing put quite a damper on my game day festivities, but I had to face facts. I had given birth to three large babies. Internal organs and tissues were not quite where they used to be, and my doctor said it was time to put them back where they belong.

When I tried to inform Francis about the procedure, he cringed, shook his head, and finally waved me off, saying, "I don't need to know the details!" Rather than seeking knowledge of the nitty gritty, he preferred to sugar-coat the facts by saying, "Yeah, my wife's going to the hospital to get her plumbing all buttoned up."

I discovered Francis's reaction was typical.

I was catching up with my brother, Tray, on the phone one day and asked what my sister-in-law, Jacq, was up to these days. Tray replied, "Well, I guess she's going to have some surgery done...."

Concerned, I interjected, "Surgery? What kind of surgery?"

After an uncomfortable pause, my brother responded, "You know, *lady surgery.*"

Ahhh. 'Nuff said.

I borrowed my brother's phrase when I had to explain why I'd be laid up for the next couple weeks, simply saying, "I'm having *lady surgery.*" The women I spoke with usually said, "Oh," tilted their heads sympathetically to the side, then offered to cook something for me. Men universally cringed and looked for the nearest escape. Either way, no further details were necessary or desired.

I never imagined I'd ever be one of those middle-aged women who would need *lady surgery.* In my twenties and thirties, I thought I was invincible.

I was proud that my five-foot-four-inch frame gave birth to nine-pound babies without drugs—stupid, I know. I figured I was "hearty stock" and could handle childbirth, heavy lifting, gutter cleaning, power washing, and lawn mowing with no repercussions.

I knew women who had to cross their legs if they laughed too hard. When the aerobics instructor at our local YMCA demanded jumping jacks, the forty-something women in the class ran to the restroom after three or four jumps. In my early forties, I started to understand their behavior, and soon, I was fighting them for an empty stall.

At first I brushed off these incidents as minor inconveniences. But a year or two down the road, I noticed the same embarrassing phenomenon happening in other situations.

I used to really enjoy a good sneeze. That tickly feeling in your nose, the slow inhale as you surrender to the natural forces of your own body, and then the spontaneous blast that leaves you feeling cleansed.

However, sneezing in my mid-forties was a whole other ball game. The tickly sensation was followed by an "uh oh," as

I scrambled to clench my legs together in a defensive posture. Inevitably, the sneeze could not be stopped, and I would be left to deal with the consequences.

Lovely.

During my forties, hearty laughter, coughing, and other normal body movements became risky business. I had to think about my actions like never before. *Mowing the lawn? Sure, why not. Moving the couch? Hmm, maybe. Jumping on the trampoline with the kids? Definitely not.*

When I began assessing my daily activities in terms of whether or not they might cause my internal organs to drop out onto the floor, I knew it was definitely time to get a medical professional involved.

My doctor allayed my fears by clearly explaining the surgical procedure with both words and rubber gloves. That talented man could take an ordinary surgical glove, and with a few twists and turns, form it into any one of the assorted female reproductive organs in order to explain my condition. It was truly amazing. I started to wonder if he worked at kids' birthday parties on weekends.

So on that ill-fated Super Bowl Sunday, with my doctor and every other red-blooded American looking forward to gobbling gallons of queso dip, I was having an entirely different kind of party getting ready for the next day's surgery. Unfortunately, the bowl that had my attention was located in my powder room.

But it was okay, I was ready for the show. I was at the line of scrimmage, I was prepared for the blitz, and I would go into overtime if necessary. I only hoped I'd make the conversion from wide receiver to tight end without too many stitches.

SEASON 4 ◆ EPISODE 4

HOW TO SUCCEED IN PARENTING BY REALLY TRYING

A couple of hours after a developmental pediatrician diagnosed three-year-old Hayden with autism spectrum disorder, we were frantically grabbing every book on the subject in the library, determined to prove the doctor wrong.

One memorable passage in an outdated book painted a grim picture of the "typical" scenario: "Parents receive the diagnosis and are determined to get their child all appropriate treatments. They are encouraged when their child makes progress with aggressive interventions. But as the child grows, the gap between him and his peers widens. As an adolescent, he wants friends, but is confused by nonverbal cues, facial expressions and gestures. Unable to develop peer relationships, he seeks the comfort of his daily routine—watching the same television shows every day and pacing around the perimeter of his back yard. The parents realize their son's delays are insurmountable and accept that he will never lead a normal life."

We put that book back on the shelf. It was the only time in our marriage I would ever see Francis cry.

This prognosis was too painful to consider, so while Hayden was young, we did whatever we could. The next eight years were a blur of home therapies, speech therapies, occupational therapies, physical therapies, gluten-free and casein-free diets, prescription vitamins, sensory integration regimens, IEP meetings, monitored peer play dates, doctor appointments, and mountains of insurance claim forms.

Fortunately, in the third grade, Hayden's doctor told us that, while he should continue to work through lingering social delays and sensory issues, he no longer fit the diagnostic criteria for autism or any other developmental disorder. We were ecstatic about Hayden's progress, but kept our lifestyle of combating autistic symptoms in place. *Just in case.*

In high school, Hayden earned varsity letters in football, became a gifted musician, took multiple Advanced Placement courses, and became an Eagle Scout.

But we still worried.

There were days when we saw autism creeping around like a phantom, threatening Hayden's future. A faraway look in his eye. The sound of him muttering to himself in the shower. His stubborn aversion to certain textures in food and clothing. Social awkwardness. His tendency to avoid interaction.

We tried to put it out of our minds and hope the ghosts of his past were simply personality traits that wouldn't stop him from forming meaningful relationships in life.

During the winter of his senior year in high school, Hayden landed the role of J.B. Biggley in the school's production of *How to Succeed in Business Without Really Trying.* We didn't know anything about the musical, and as usual, Hayden was not forthcoming with any details.

He arrived home late from nightly practices, grunted his usual brief greeting, and retreated to his room. He seemed intent on keeping his involvement a secret, and although we worried if he was okay, we did our best to respect his privacy.

We arrived on the night of the first show, without a clue about what was in store.

As we bought our tickets and found our seats, several parents accosted us, gasping, "Your son is the one playing J.B. Biggley?! He is amazing! He steals the show!" Knowing Hayden's lack of interpersonal skills, we thought they might be mistaking his personality for character acting. However, when he made his appearance on stage, we understood what everyone was talking about.

Simply put, Hayden blew everyone away.

We were shocked when Hayden took the stage and portrayed J.B. Biggley with expert character acting, complete with hilarious facial expressions and a bold stage acting voice. Although Hayden had always had advanced music skills, we didn't know that he also had a perfectly pitched singing voice, and apparently neither did his classmates who cheered and hooted when Hayden belted out "Grand Old Ivy." Those of us who knew Hayden nearly fell out of our seats when he performed a little soft shoe with Biggley's love interest, Hedy, then crooned "Love from a Heart of Gold" to her with perfect tenor's vibrato. Despite his heavy linebacker frame, Hayden danced so gracefully, twirling Hedy before kneeling before her and setting her gently on his knee.

How had he hidden all this talent from us for so long?

At the curtain call, the actors took their turns bowing to the audience. When Hayden stepped up and bent at the waist, the crowd jumped to its feet, giving him the loudest standing ovation. *No one knows he was once diagnosed with autism*, I thought, my eyes brimming with tears.

Sitting back in our seats in total disbelief, it was as if all our years of hard work had come to fruition. Like comprehending the vastness of the infinite cosmos, my mind was boggled by the magnitude of Hayden's potential and the promise of his happy future.

SEASON 4 ◆ EPISODE 5

THE AVOCADO
AND GOLDEN RULE

Facing Lilly's fall semester parent-teacher conference, I found myself feeling guilty...again.

"Hello, Mrs. Molinari," the teachers would always start, shuffling through files to find records pertaining to my child. "I'm sure you've been keeping up with [Hayden's/Anna's/Lilly's] grades on the online parent portal and know that [he/she] turned several assignments in late this term."

Every time, I'd stare like a deer in the headlights. *Oh shoot! I forgot to check that online portal thingy again...where the heck did I write down the username and password?* I'd respond, "Yes, of course, I check the parent portal frequently, and I am *very* concerned. Obviously, if I had been informed of these assignments, I would have *certainly* made sure that [Hayden/ Anna/Lilly] had turned them in on time."

"But Mrs. Molinari," the teachers would inevitably retort while I braced myself to be exposed as a fraud, "All the assignments are listed in advance on our class website and teachers' blogs...You know that, right?"

"Well, certainly!" I'd lie, desperately scanning my brain for some kind of excuse for my parental neglect. But inevitably, like some kind of over-aged juvenile delinquent who'd been cornered, I'd cower to the teacher's authority and take the blame.

I'd admit not checking the parent portal as often as I should. I'd concede never reading the teachers' blogs. I'd divulge I didn't know the class website address. I'd confess to never joining the parents' Facebook group, using the class hashtag, or following the school updates on Instagram.

I'd acknowledge I hadn't figured out how to open the progress reports on Google Drive, and I'd reveal I was totally clueless about the "cloud" thingamabob that everyone keeps talking about.

I'd plead for forgiveness and promise that from here on out, I'd be good.

I'd sulk out of parent-teacher conferences and combat my shame with self-pity, pointing out that our parents never had to worry about checking online grade portals and teacher blogs.

In the seventies, our parents came home from an honest day's work in their gabardine slacks, had a satisfying dinner of Swiss steak and canned peas, then retired to the den to relax with a vodka gimlet and a riveting episode of *Gunsmoke*.

After cleaning tables and washing dishes, we kids were expected to finish our homework with minimal supervision. If our book bags contained graded papers or report cards, we were expected to hand-deliver these items to our parents. There was no need for them to snuff out their cigarettes or get up from their avocado and gold lounge furniture, much less remember complicated website addresses and passwords. All they had to do was glance down at the papers in their polyester-draped laps during the Chiffon margarine commercials.

If the grades were bad, we got a lecture and were not allowed to go out and play. If the grades were good, our parents put the papers on our refrigerators with magnets.

Back in those days, parenting seemed straightforward: set clear expectations for kids, praise their accomplishments, and let the school do its job. I found myself, once again, longing for a simpler time. Clearly, roles had changed. Teachers created and assigned work, not only for students but also for parents, who were now expected to research, monitor, and enforce the details of assignments and grade progress.

I couldn't be sure which parental role was better for our kids, but I couldn't help wishing I'd been born a generation ago.

I admitted I was lousy at managing my kids' school assignments, but I thought, *if only it were the 1970s, I would have been the perfect mother.* I would have been quite comfortable wearing a Dacron sweater-vest and gauchos. I would have had fun whipping up zippy casseroles using Spanish olives, cottage cheese, and frankfurters. I would have really enjoyed a simple evening watching *BJ and the Bear* on a console television. Minus the cigarettes, that is.

SEASON 4 ◆ EPISODE 6

POMP AND UNUSUAL CIRCUMSTANCES

By the time the head of the school got to the graduates whose names started with an "M," my feet were bloody stumps. I thought I'd be fine in two-inch sling backs, but an hour into the ceremony, my toe knuckles were raw, and the pointed heels sunk into the grass under the enormous tent.

I got up from our reserved row of seats to get a better vantage point to take photographs. Our motley crew of relatives—Anna, Lilly, aunts, grandmothers, an uncle, a cousin, and Francis, who had already spilled coffee on his tie—had all come to see Hayden receive his high school diploma. We looked the same as the other families seated around us, but somehow I felt like our family was different.

This school was Hayden's third high school in four years. Our navy family was required to move after his ninth-grade year at an American high school on an army post in Germany, to an inner-city public school in Florida, and finally to Rhode Island where Hayden finished his senior year at Portsmouth Abbey, a local boarding school. We were surprised when he was accepted to the school as a day student, and we were elated when the school offered us enough financial aid to make it affordable on our tight military budget.

At the Abbey's preseason football camp, Hayden made his

debut as the new senior. He was quirky, husky, and lacked the personal hygiene skills necessary to keep up with the school's strict dress code. A sort of "nutty professor" type.

In past schools, our unusual son was received with mixed reviews. In Germany, the students saw him as smart and uniquely funny—someone everyone wanted to know. In Florida, he was perceived as odd, and over two years he didn't develop any close friendships. When he started at the Abbey, I wondered if the predominantly wealthy, preppy boarding school students would look beyond the surface to appreciate Hayden's distinctive sense of humor and extraordinary intellect.

Throughout the year, we had mixed clues to Hayden's reputation at the Abbey. The football coach smiled widely when speaking about him; however, the English teacher grimaced when describing the "odd British accent of questionable origin" Hayden employed when reciting poetry. The students and faculty reported that he "stole the show" in the winter musical; however, of the four boys that Hayden invited to our house for his April birthday party, only one showed up.

The head of school called the next graduate: "Ellen Mangino."

Several students stood to cheer on their graduating friend. As I wobbled on painful shoes up the rows with my camera, my mind raced with random thoughts. *These students have had four years to bond. Hayden wasn't here long enough to be understood.*

"Sean McDonald." More applause as I inched closer to the stage.

Has our military lifestyle robbed our son of the opportunity to form close relationships with his peers? Does he think that it's his fault?

"Julian Miller." I raised the camera to my eyes with shaking hands and waited for Hayden's name to be called.

"Hayden Clark Molinari." I snapped the shutter repeatedly, catching glimpses through the viewfinder of my son making his way through the crowd of navy-jacketed students to the smiling headmaster. In a fog of emotion, I could not coordinate the still images I saw with my eyes with what I distinctly heard with my ears.

I took the camera away for a moment and realized, *They are giving him a standing ovation.*

Students and teachers leapt to their feet to cheer for an unusual boy who had been with them for nine short months. Through the din of applause and shouts, I managed to take a dozen more photographs before bursting into tears.

Minutes later, the students spilled out of the tent, milling around in a sort of preppy mosh pit in the bright sunlight. Fighting the celebratory crowd, we found Hayden amongst the jovial graduates, slapping each other's backs.

He smiled broadly as I kissed his prickly cheek, silently reminding him, *You will always be loved.*

SEASON 4 ◆ EPISODE 7

LIFE, HOT FLASHING
BEFORE MY EYES

On the morning of my forty-eighth birthday, I had my very first hot flash.

The uncanny coincidence of this occurrence made it seem psychosomatic. However, I could not deny the unsettling reality of the sweat mustache that had formed while I was eating my scrambled eggs. I tried to pass the event off as a fluke, but while going about my day, I started thinking, *You know, I'm getting kind of old. Really old.*

I had always been content with the progression of my life as a wife and mother of three; generally gratified to have found a calling to serve my family, rather than having my own career and choosing where I'd like to live. I said many times, "As long as the kids are happy, I'm happy."

But suddenly, life was passing before my eyes as if death were imminent. I thought about my education and quickly decided I'd wasted it. I thought about my early work experiences as a young attorney before navy life, and I summarily concluded my brain had atrophied from lack of use and must now be the size of a tangerine. I thought about my homemaking skills, swiftly determining I was mediocre at best.

After decades of gleaning my own identity from the contentment of my family members, it was suddenly *all about me.*

There was something about this particular birthday that had me wallowing in panicked self-loathing. Perhaps it was the hair that seemed to be clinging damply to the back of my perspiring neck. Or maybe it was the lack of bladder control. Did I detect a throbbing bunion? Was I sprouting age spots?

As the day progressed, I relentlessly berated, harangued, nit-picked, criticized, and condemned myself until I could feel my spider veins bulge.

Why do I snap at the kids so much? Why can't I seem to cook a decent meal without turning meat into shoe leather? Why do I watch so much TV at night? Why couldn't I ever get rid of this paunch? Why didn't I moisturize when I was younger? Why do I always forget to bring my coupons to the commissary? Why? Why? Why?!

By the time Francis came home from work, I was slumped in a kitchen chair, staring into a cup of coffee gone cold.

I'd hit bottom.

"Happy birthday, Honey!" he offered with a grin. I looked up weakly, and said, "I think I'm having some kind of mid-life crisis...can you sit down and listen to me for a sec?" For the next twenty minutes, Francis sat calmly in his cammies at our kitchen table, permitting me to tell him all about the hot flash and the resulting epiphany revealing the harsh truth: I had never really amounted to much and it was definitely too late to do anything about it.

Francis waited until the end of my rant, then simply got up and poured us each a glass of wine. I wondered whether he had heard anything I'd just said. Then, holding his glass up to toast mine, he delivered the birthday joke that had become his annual tradition: "Honey, you might have turned forty-eight today, but you're built like you're forty-seven!"

I couldn't help but laugh like I always do, and in that instant, my hot flash turned into a flash flood of gratitude for the ups and downs of life, the simplicity of love, and the boundless support of my little family.

SEASON 4 ◆ EPISODE 8

THE SILENT TREATMENT

I'd always been the kind of person who had to fill awkward silences. Someone who couldn't tell a story without all the excruciating details, who chatted endlessly at social gatherings, then woke up the next morning, slapped my forehead and said, "Me and my big mouth."

I never understood why I was that way. If every human personality trait from narcissism to the Oedipus complex has its roots in childhood, I surmised that was when it all started.

My father, William Durwood Smith, Jr., who was shipped off to Fork Union Military Academy at the tender age of ten, was determined to be a more hands-on parent than his own had been. If my brother or I disobeyed our father, he simply selected from a variety of corporal punishments that were considered perfectly appropriate, if not advisable. No one would have batted a powder-blue frosted eyelid back then if a parent gave his kid a whack on the tush for saying she didn't walk the dog because she was in the middle of a particularly riveting episode of *Diff'rent Strokes*, or if she called her brother a "ginormous butt-face" while in line at Mister Donut.

My dad also had a repertoire of noncorporal punishments, such as making us sit at the dinner table until every last bite of those lima beans was gone, being grounded for coming home twenty minutes after Mom rang the bell, and having to confess to the neighbor that I dug for worms in her front lawn.

But there was one form of punishment I considered worse than a lashing with Durwood's infamous three-inch white vinyl belt.

It was the dreaded Silent Treatment.

When my father would refuse to acknowledge my presence for a period of hours or days, I had time to ponder the offense for which I was being punished, but also I had plenty of time to feel regret for the thirty-seven other things I'd screwed up in the past. It was sheer agony.

I would have volunteered to walk barefoot over a bed of bumblebees, run through a thicket of thorn bushes, or take a carrot peeler to my shins if only my father would just speak to me again.

Thus, when I became an adult, I couldn't stand silence.

So when Francis and I stopped speaking to each other right before a twelve-hour drive home from our family vacation, I found it particularly difficult. We had both had it. He'd had it with my extended family with whom we'd just spent two weeks in a tiny beach cottage, and I'd had it with him for having had it with my family.

We went to bed angry the night before, backs to each other, vowing *See how he/she likes this—I'm not going to say a word!* At six the next morning, we hit the road in silence. The kids, oblivious to our temporary marital discord, slept soundly.

All across North Carolina, I sat arms crossed, staring bitterly out the passenger's side window. In Virginia, I kept quiet, comforting myself with a small neck pillow. In Maryland, I dozed off. In Delaware, I couldn't specifically recall why we stopped talking to each other in the first place. By the time we got to New Jersey, I just wanted us to be normal again.

"Are we going to get something to eat?" I croaked, my vocal

cords showing signs of atrophy after six hours of silence. "Yeah, in just a few minutes," Francis said, his soft tone indicating he wanted normalcy too.

After hoagies off the Garden State Parkway, we climbed back into our luggage-laden minivan for the remainder of our trip home. In New York, we chatted about the news. In Connecticut, we were quiet again, only because we were tired.

Finally home in Rhode Island, it was clear that our Silent Treatment had been a blessing rather than a punishment. In the absence of words, we had time to regret. And to miss each other.

Sometimes, silence is golden.

SEASON 4 ◆ EPISODE 9

FRESHMAN ORIENTATION AND OTHER ALIEN MIND TRICKS

Our son, Hayden, was abducted by aliens. Strange creatures from a far-off land lured him to their institution, garbed him in their apparel, and claimed him as their own.

To make matters worse, he went with them willingly.

Francis and I agreed, through a complex combination of loans, financial aid, the GI Bill, and possibly human sacrifice, to pay these aliens sixty-four thousand dollars a year to keep him.

No, we hadn't fallen prey to a Vulcan mind-meld. The Galactic Empire had not injected us with the RNA brainwashing virus. We had not been hypnotized by Sleestaks from *Land of the Lost*. We merely took Hayden to his college orientation.

When we arrived, they immediately separated us from Hayden, whisking him off with the other starry-eyed newcomers to "start a memorable and important time in their academic and professional journeys." We knew they really intended to erase our son's memory. Eighteen years of hard work down the drain.

In order to placate the parents, they pumped us full of coffee, plied us with shiny new pens, and herded us around to "informative sessions" such as "Letting Go" and "Money Matters" in a suspiciously spaceship-shaped building they referred to as "EMPAC"—The Experimental Media and Performing Arts Center.

While the parents were locked in the EMPAC mothership with the institution's leaders, our children were off playing ice breaker games with legions of bubbly upperclassmen dressed in matching college t-shirts and well-worn sneakers. The incoming freshmen were encouraged to become independent, to make all decisions without involving their parents, other than to send them the bills.

The institution's leaders tried to allay our fears, characterizing the terrifying experience of handing over our flesh and blood to complete strangers as a normal rite of passage. They told us not to be concerned, because our children would have all sorts of advisors to guide them. There would be Student Orientation Advisors, Resident Advisors, Academic Advisors, Graduate Assistants, Learning Assistants, and Peer Tutors. But all we were thinking was, "Yeah, but who's going to tell him to wear his retainer?"

They said our kids would be well-nourished with a variety of meal plans ranging from "unlimited access" otherwise known as the "fast-track-to-morbid-obesity" plan, to the "custom plan" commonly referred to as the "go-broke-on-take-out-after-you-expend-your-dining-hall-allotment" plan.

Rest assured, they told us, the students would never go hungry thanks to an impossibly confusing supplemental system of "flex dollars" and "student advantage dollars" which could be used to buy an endless array of well-balanced meals (READ: pizza, chocolate milk, and potato chips) all over campus twenty-four seven.

They paraded a series of experts from the health clinic and campus security before us, telling us that without our adult children's express consents, we were not permitted to know if they got arrested or pregnant. And lastly, we were informed we had no right to access our children's grades, despite the fact we had to take second mortgages on our homes to pay the tuition.

Finally, we were released into the blinding sunlight to find our newly-indoctrinated children milling about the quad. In order to squeeze every last dollar from our increasingly shallow pockets, we were funneled through the campus bookstore, where we bought Hayden a lanyard with a hook large enough to hold his student ID, military ID, room key, bike lock key, asthma inhaler, a bottle of hand sanitizer, a stick of lip balm, a thumb drive, and—most importantly—a framed eight-by-ten photograph of me, his mother.

Six short weeks later, we surrendered Hayden to this alien academic institution, hoping he would heed the words of a well-known extraterrestrial and always remember to phone home.

SEASON 4 ◆ EPISODE 10

TEEN TERMS

One night Francis and I were in the family room, mesmerized by a shameless reality show, when suddenly there was a rumbling down the staircase.

"Mom! Dad! Mom! Dad! Mom! Dad!" Anna, sputtered, while jumping up and down in front of us.

"What is it, Anna?!" I shouted, half expecting her hair to be on fire.

"He asked me to hang out! He asked me to hang out! He asked me to hang out!" Anna yelled while fist-pumping into the air.

"*Who* asked you to, to... to hang out, and what do you mean, 'hang out'?"

Still surging with pent-up excitement, Anna grabbed the arm of the couch, and repeatedly kicked both feet behind her. "Matt! Matt! Matt asked me to hang out!" she answered between donkey kicks.

We already knew all about Matt. In fact, every day for the last few months, we'd been hearing Anna talk about this boy: how cute he was, how he would come to the art room to talk to her after school, how great the article was that he wrote for the school newspaper, how he was named Athlete of the Week, how he danced with her at the holiday ball, how he kissed her in the theater costume closet, yada, yada, yada.

"Oh," Francis chimed in, "you mean he *finally* asked you out on a real date?"

Oh, jeez. I wish he hadn't said that. For the next twenty minutes, Anna rolled her eyes and sighed while trying to explain why he was not her boyfriend and they were certainly not going on a date. "We're just hanging out!" Anna said with one last spasmodic flail of arms and legs, before running off to get dolled up to meet Matt.

Apparently, teen romance as we knew it had changed completely. Unbeknownst to us, the terms "boyfriend" and "girlfriend" were used only when two teenagers were very "serious." Until then, they were to be referred to as "talking." When one talking teen asked his corresponding talking teen to go out with him to a restaurant or movie, this was most definitely not a date. This was called "hanging out."

But "hanging out" was not to be confused with "hooking up," which, our kids assured us, did not mean what it did back in the eighties. Regardless, it likely included acts in which our teenage daughter should not engage unless she wanted to be grounded for life.

We also learned that parents were to refrain from referring to kissing as "making out," "mashing," "frenching," or "necking," which modern teenagers considered as antiquated as butterfly clips and Beanie Babies.

Anna eventually reappeared in the family room, all glossed up and ready to go on her non-date with her non-boyfriend. Francis drove her to the base gate and got out of the car to introduce himself to Matt. After shaking hands, Francis looked the boy directly in the eye for a moment, communicating without the need for words: *Regardless of what terms you're using these days, we've all been there, and we know exactly what you're up to.*

SEASON 4 ◆ EPISODE 11

TEARS ON MY TOOTHBRUSH

It didn't hit me until I saw the smear of toothpaste on the sink that morning.

I'd heard the stories before. *I cried for an hour in the bathtub... I couldn't get out of bed for a week... I was a snotty, puffy-eyed mess... I didn't think I'd make it to Thanksgiving.*

I listened with genuine compassion to fellow moms, but I couldn't personally relate. Those things would never happen to me.

Then, we dropped Hayden off at college.

"He's only going to be three hours away," I told a friend. "And besides, a little separation will be good for all of us. I won't be one of those people who blubbers like a baby."

"Oh, you will," my friend warned. "Trust me."

We helped him set up his dorm room with plastic bins, granola bars, power strips, extra sticks of deodorant, clip on lamps, new sheets that won't be washed this semester, and cheapo particle board shelving that threatened to buckle like a ramen noodle under the weight of the tiny microwave.

Dry-eyed as planned, I kissed his prickly cheek goodbye at four o'clock, so he could go to his first hall meeting and we could wolf down free hors d'oeuvres at the parent reception. After more than our share of chicken bites and veggies drenched in ranch,

Francis and I spent a couple of carefree days exploring the nearby lakes of Upstate New York.

I awoke early the first morning back home, after getting home late the night before. I could've used another twenty minutes of sleep, but Francis needed a ride to the airport for a work trip, so I shuffled my way to our bathroom down the hall.

I looked bleary-eyed into the bathroom mirror at my pillow-crimped bangs and groped for my toothbrush. Glancing down, I saw Francis's toothbrush. And mine. But where Hayden's toothbrush had been, there was only a smear.

A smear that, up until that point, had always irritated me. *Why do men refuse to thoroughly rinse the slobbery toothpaste out of their toothbrushes? Don't they care that someone has to continuously clean the dried-up smears off the sink?*

But this time, I wasn't annoyed. I stared at the smear, and it hit me.

He's gone.

I felt a hot sting behind my eyes and a flush in my cheeks. In a stupor, I left the bathroom and found myself at the open door of Hayden's room.

How sweet...his unmade bed! I gulped and pulled a tissue from a box on his nightstand. *Oh, and that odor of teenage boy sweat.* I breathed in deeply. *He never did take that bowl down to the kitchen like I asked.* I smiled at the three-day-old tomato-sauce-enameled dish and let a tear tumble down my cheek.

I explored Hayden's abandoned room, noting every void in the dust where books, alarm clocks, and speakers used to be. I inventoried the vestiges—gum wrappers, crumbs, pennies, and tiny tumbleweeds of God-knows-what. All the things that had once been bones of contention were now cherished relics of the time—now past—when Hayden lived under the same roof with us.

And then, I gave in to the parental prerogative I had denied myself based upon logic and reason, and I bawled like a baby.

Is it Thanksgiving yet?

SEASON 4 ◆ EPISODE 12

PUPPY PERSONALITY DISORDER

Once upon a time, my life was normal. I showered regularly. I ran errands. I cooked and cleaned. I watched TV. I slept in a bed.

Until one day, Francis and I drove from our home in Rhode Island to a cranberry farm in Massachusetts and picked up a wriggling ball of fur that changed everything.

We felt a twinge of guilt taking an eight-week-old Labrador retriever away from his littermates, with whom he had spent his days snuggling and tussling. But ever since the death a few months earlier of our beloved Dinghy, the dog who saw us through deployments, military moves, and an overseas tour, we knew our family needed another dog. So we wrapped the puppy in a blanket and nuzzled him all the way home, happily ignorant of the chaos about to ensue.

We named him Moby, a tribute to our tour of duty in nautical New England. However, other apt titles occurred to us that week, as we learned the multiple facets of our new puppy's complex personality.

Puddle Maker christened every rug in our house, and we considering buying stock in puppy training pads. Kibble Gobbler inhaled scoops of puppy food as if he were a starving prisoner, usually with one paw plopping in his water dish. Spawn of Cujo had an active period after meals, involving relentless ankle biting, broom chasing, and upholstery shredding. During this time, we couldn't approach Staple Gun for fear that what might seem like a sweet lick on the nose would turn out to be a needle-teeth lancing of the sensitive area just inside our nostrils.

Sweater Snagger sunk his fishhook nails into us when we carried him down the porch steps for potty time. Although he seemed to know what was expected of him, Little Con Artist enjoyed delaying the potty process long enough that we were forced to stand out in the cold while he innocently played in the mud.

After following me around the house biting my shoes, Limp Noodle insisted on taking a nap while laying over my feet. I sat motionless so as to not incite further mayhem, while the housework didn't get done, food didn't get cooked, and I didn't shower. This was generally the time our base neighbors came by to see the newest member of our family. They all remarked how calm Little Faker was and asked me why I looked so bedraggled.

After the fourth night sleeping on the floor beside the dog crate, I needed a break from the Puppet Master. Just like the dog training book instructed, I gave him a special treat and put him in the playpen we'd assembled in the kitchen. I praised him, closed the gate, and left to drive the girls to school.

Fifteen minutes later, my neighbor called. "What are you doing to that poor dog?!" he cried, explaining that he could hear incessant yelping through the walls of our shared duplex.

I rushed home to find that Mr. Passive Aggressive "made a deposit" in his playpen in protest over being left alone. Canine Picasso also smeared it all over the floor, rug, dog bed, gate, toys, and himself. I spent the rest of the morning scrubbing and disinfecting, and although everything looked clean, we considered deworming the children, just in case.

At first, I thought Moby was the one with the personality disorder, but then realized it was me who'd lost a grip on reality.

I'd transformed from navy mom to Pin Cushion, Pooper Scooper, Feed Bag, and Canine Concierge. I was so delusional that, despite baggy eyes, multiple puncture wounds, and a complete loss of hygiene standards, I had been utterly blinded by love.

SEASON 4 ◆ EPISODE 13

THE TWELVE TAKES
OF CHRISTMAS

"C'mon everybody!" I bellowed from our living room, "Let's get this over with!"

"KIDS!? HONEY!?" I yelled from behind my camera, which was precariously perched on top of an Anthony's Seafood matchbook, two beer coasters, three *National Geographic* magazines, *Roget's Thesaurus*, and our coffee table, at the precise trajectory needed to capture a centered image of our family of five and the dog in front of the fireplace.

Knowing the tiniest slip of the hand (or the dog's tail) might ruin my painstakingly calibrated line of sight, I was reluctant to abandon my post. But when no one responded to my wails, I marched off to find them.

Twenty minutes later, I had managed to drag the resistant members of my family into the living room. Francis was miffed I forced him to abandon a particularly riveting rerun of *House Hunters*. Hayden was annoyed that he had to pause Dragon Warrior VII just as he was about to master Ranger class. Anna couldn't fathom what was so important that she had to stop texting the cute boy from her statistics class. Lilly was pouting about being torn away from Snapchat.

They were all sporting major attitudes, but it was now or never.

"Listen! I don't like this any more than you do, but our family and friends have come to expect a Molinari family photo Christmas card every year, so backs straight! Stomachs tight! And get happy, dammit!"

My moping gaggle huddled together on the fireplace hearth, in shared irritation over being forced to pose for a family photo. "Leave a spot for me on the left, and smile!" I ordered from behind my camera.

I gingerly jabbed the camera's timer button, careful not to knock the lens from its matchbook-coaster-thesaurus tripod, then leapt like an overweight gazelle, across our faux oriental rug, and into my designated position.

"Mom, the camera's blinking."

"Honey, when do you want us to smile?"

"Are you sure you pressed the button, Mom?"

"I don't KNOW!" I screeched through my grinning clenched teeth, "Just keep smiling!"

"But, isn't it supposed to fla..."

It flashed.

It took two more takes before we realized the camera flashed after a prescribed series of slow and fast blinks. Hayden sneezed in the middle of take number four. The phone rang during take number five. I blinked in take number six. We all got the giggles in take number seven, when Francis belched up a pungent odor reminiscent of Genoa salami.

We finally realized we forgot to include the dog, Moby, and it took two takes, three pieces of cheese, and a tennis ball before he would agree to sit. Somewhere along the way, I inadvertently nudged the June 2009 issue of *National Geographic*, and it took me twenty minutes and three more ruined takes to get the family centered in the viewfinder again.

On take number thirteen, we were so desperate to end our torturous holiday photo odyssey, we all agreed to cooperate to take one final, flawless shot.

With my last ounce of patience, I tapped the button with catlike precision, and pounced into position, tipping my jaw forward to hide my double chin. The kids replaced their reluctant fake grins with genuine sparkling smiles. Francis leaned behind me to hide his now sweat-stained armpit and mustered a charming pose.

Moby sat, in perfect obedience, his ears handsomely perked.

Like the townspeople of Bethlehem, we looked for the bright light that would finally bring us salvation.

"Why didn't it flash?" Francis whispered.

After another minute, Lilly extracted herself from our frozen pose, to check the camera.

Peering at the digital display, she read aloud, "Change battery pack."

Realizing that a flawless family photo was never going to happen, we decided one of the twelve takes would have to do, because reality is as perfect as a family gets.

SEASON 4 ◆ EPISODE 14

THE DIETER'S WALL

About two weeks into my diet, I realized I was starving, and no low-cal protein snack would stave off my hunger pangs. Although pork products sounded mouthwateringly delicious in my weakened state, I eventually determined that the diet was a bunch of baloney. No matter how many times some rich television celebrity—who probably ate diet meals prepared by her personal chef and had a trainer who comes to her home gym—told me "the pounds just melt away," I doubted that any diet would work for me.

The first few days of my diet had seemed like fun. The same way raking leaves seemed fun for the first fifteen minutes until I realized it was going to take five hours and I'd have to do it every weekend. Or the way cooking dinner seemed like fun when I was first married, but then twenty years later, I would rather chew my own arm off than prepare another meal. Or the way running seemed like fun until I came to the end of the second block and suddenly felt as if my heart might explode.

By the end of the second week of dieting, I wanted someone to hit me in the head with a frying pan—preferably one that had just fried up a dozen crisp slices of bacon—to put me out of my misery.

I hit the wall one day while shopping at the commissary. The satiating effect of the protein shake I'd guzzled that morning had worn off, and I was beginning to feel that familiar grumbling in the pit of my stomach. I was most definitely hungry.

I rushed from my minivan, across the blustery commissary parking lot, and into the store. Everything was fine in produce, where I followed my grocery list to a tee, except for the bagged Lite Caesar Salad Kit I decided would make a satisfying diet lunch.

The burning in my innards was unnoticeable at first, but it slowly built as I weaved through the grocery aisles. I made it through the canned goods, baking supplies, and cereal without incident, but as my hunger mounted, things began to unravel in the snack food aisle. With each step, the burning in my gut seared deeper, until I was ready to grab a cheese ball out of the dairy case and eat it like an apple, cellophane and all. I resisted my urges, but soon I felt as if I might implode like the collapsing core of a supernova, transforming the entire commissary into a giant black hole and destroying civilization as we know it.

That's when it happened. Lying there, on the shelf beside the display of Pringles, I saw it. Some coupon clipper had generously left me a lifeline. "One dollar off five cans," it read. It was such a fantastic deal, it seemed almost compulsory. Saliva dripped from my lower lip as I loaded the Pringles into my cart.

By the time I approached the check-out area, I had grabbed Oreos, frozen pizza, apple turnovers, and a one-pound block of cheddar cheese. Blinded by desperation, I caught the tantalizing aroma of roasted chicken.

Two rotisserie chickens soon joined the mountain of forbidden foods heaped onto the cashier's conveyor belt. While the bagger loaded my groceries into the back of the minivan, I fantasized about sneaking food to the front seat for the drive home. Not a new ploy, and not only fantasy.

I recalled telling unsuspecting baggers I needed to put a rotisserie chicken up in the front seat to keep it warm, knowing

I just wanted to sneak a piece on the way home. I'd pull into my driveway, my face and steering wheel slick with grease, and a drumstick clenched between my teeth.

But on the day I hit the wall, the miracle of convenience foods helped me to stick to my diet. I managed to make it home from the commissary, where I frantically dug through the grocery bags in the trunk of my minivan to find that salad kit. I stumbled into the house without unloading my groceries, faint with hunger, and devoured the salad out of a Tupperware bowl while standing at the kitchen counter.

Hail, Caesar.

SEASON 4 ◆ EPISODE 15

THE OTHER MEN (AND A FEW WOMEN) IN MY LIFE

In my years as a military spouse, I regularly had relationships with people other than Francis. Often several times a day. Some were veritable strangers to me, while others were men I had come to know quite well. And, believe it or not, a few of them were women.

Most of these relationships were light and friendly, a few were all-business, but all had a certain intimacy. It may have appeared that we were mere acquaintances but—make no mistake about it—they peered deeply into my psyche, and they knew my secrets.

These men and women were the military base gate guards.

As my minivan inched forward in the line toward the base gate, I was unsuspecting. I chewed my gum. I listened to the radio. I glanced down at my commissary list. I casually plucked a flosser or tweezers from my console and used the flip-down mirror to groom myself, unconcerned that the gate guard was about to peek into the intimate corners of my life.

"Hi! How're you today?" I asked after stopping at the guard shack. I fumbled for my ID, which was always jammed too far into the pocket of my wallet. "Darnit," I muttered, licking my thumb in order to get a decent grip on the plastic.

"There you go!" I finally produced my ID, hoping he won't scrutinize the black and white photo taken the day my hairdryer broke last year. Without a word, he accepted my ID. After swiping it through his hand-held scanner, he stared at the ID and the machine's display. Back and forth, back and forth, analyzing whatever had been revealed.

All at once, I felt vulnerable, exposed, guilty for something I hadn't done.

He looked directly at my face, too. I smiled nervously. *What is he thinking? Is he trying to match my double chin to the one in my ID picture?*

He leaned over a bit and inspected the interior of my minivan. His flashlight scanned each row of seats, the floor mats, the dark spaces under the dash. His eyes paused a moment on Moby, panting and seated in the second row on a furry blanket.

I saw the corner of his mouth rise a little, and I detected a reaction in his eyes. *Is it a twinkle?*

There were several times over the years when the gate guard ordered me to pull my van over so he could conduct a random vehicle search. Without a doubt, random vehicle searches took our relationship to another level.

In these instances, I followed the gate guard's orders to exit my van and got ready for him to pat me down. But instead of frisking me, he directed me to stand aside and watch, while he searched every inch of my vehicle, looking under my hood and using mirrors to peek up my undercarriage.

Once, while stationed in Germany, the guard even had his drug detecting shepherd sniff the junk in my trunk.

On one hand, I was always embarrassed when he shone his flashlight into every nook and cranny—I would have preferred it with the lights off—but at the same time, I desperately sought his approval.

"You're good to go, Ma'am, have a nice day," I heard countless times after our little encounters. I smiled and wished him well, until next time.

As I headed for the commissary to buy turkey burgers and fiber supplements, I knew between us there were no illusions, no commitments, no secrets. The gate guard had looked into the intimate details of my life, and he was fully satisfied.

SEASON 4 ◆ EPISODE 16

SNACKS IN THE CITY

"Do you want that apple now?" I asked Anna, for the third time since boarding the train to New York City. I brought her favorite snack in my backpack, hoping a Granny Smith might keep my temperamental teen satisfied on our trip to visit colleges.

"*No*, Mom," Anna huffed, "I told you, I'm *not* hungry."

As I turned toward the window, my mind wandered to a decade ago when Anna, our fiercely independent middle child, disappeared.

She was one of those kids who would go off with a box of toys and play for hours. Francis or I would find her somewhere in our house, surrounded by her characters, her huge brown eyes flitting from one to the other, her wee lips muttering their voices in her imagined scenario.

On one particular occasion, she'd been off playing by herself so long, I became concerned.

"Anna?!" I bellowed, hoping to find her in a corner, lost in a complex drama involving Buzz Lightyear, Polly Pockets, and My Little Pony. Just as my mothering instinct was about to mobilize a grid search of our entire neighborhood, I heard something in the bonus room over our garage.

Sure enough, there she was, sitting in a heap of paper, pencils, yarn, fabric, and my sewing basket dumped upside down. "Lookit what I made, Mom," she coughed out, her voice box sluggish from hours of dormancy.

Anna, age eight, held up her creation, a full-length garment of white fleece. After making sketches in a Hello Kitty notebook, she settled on a sleek one-shoulder design with an elegant neckline and fitted skirt. Anna modeled her gown for us, and we looked on in amazement at the sophisticated silhouette and meticulous hand-stitching. Apparently, Anna had seen someone do it on TV, and was now determined to be a fashion designer.

Nearly ten years later, we were on our way to the Big Apple to follow Anna's dream.

Sitting beside my seventeen-year-old daughter, I still saw her big brown eyes flitting, lost in thought. Intuitively, I knew she was envisioning what it would be like to be a fashion design student in NYC, walking city streets in stylish outfits, sketching on sunlight-dappled park benches, and hailing cabs to meet friends for lunch in SoHo.

My baggy brown eyes were flitting too, but I was imagining rat-infested alleys, marauding pick-pocketers, subway stairwells reeking of urine, and catcalling ne'er-do-wells. Francis and I would much rather send our daughter to college somewhere in rural Vermont or Wisconsin, where sleepy campus police officers busy themselves writing citations for spitting on the sidewalk. But we knew Anna must see for herself.

Emerging from the subterranean chaos of Penn Station, we began our two-day odyssey. Piles of old snow were melting, revealing a winter's worth of grit, grime, and garbage. Dirty water dripped from scaffoldings and fire escapes above us, sometimes landing in our hair. The subway stations were a hideous cornucopia of acrid odors and filthy corners piled with discarded cigarette butts.

The housewife in me wanted to spray the whole place with bleach and give it a good scrubbing. Anna, on the other hand, was mortified her mother acted like a quintessential tourist, fiddling clumsily with my maps and subway diagrams, stopping every few blocks to mutter, "Now, which street is this?"

Despite her embarrassment, we managed to visit all the fashion design schools in Manhattan and Brooklyn in two days, using only a Metrocard, one twelve-dollar cab ride, and just under 42,000 Fitbit steps. After our last tour at Parsons School of Design, Anna slumped over a chair in the admissions office, sore, tired, and overwhelmed with the realities of the big city college experience.

I thought I'd be relieved if Anna was disappointed with urban life, but my parental instinct to protect my daughter from danger was tempered by my need to support her dreams.

"Hey, you want that apple now?" I offered, groping in my backpack. As I handed over the once flawlessly crisp Granny Smith, I saw it had become a mushy, oozing ball of bruises. I tossed it in the trash and improvised.

"Whaddya say we take a cab and go get chocolate shakes?" I said. "I know a great place on the Upper East Side." As we walked out into bustling Greenwich Village, I realized that no matter where my daughter's aspirations take her, she'll always be the apple of my eye.

SEASON 4 ◆ EPISODE 17

THE FIX IS IN

I told the folks at the local dog park they wouldn't be seeing Moby, our yellow Lab, for a couple of weeks. When I explained why, the men in the group collectively cringed and hitched their knees together.

The appointment was first thing Monday morning.

Moby loped out our front door into the crisp morning air just like always, his stout wagging tail on one end and a big sloppy smile on the other. I opened the minivan's hatch door, and Moby hopped right in. He probably thought we were driving to the beach to chase balls and eat dead fish.

But instead we took a longer trip, twenty-five minutes northward. I pulled into the closest available parking space at the veterinary clinic, jumped out, and opened the back door.

"Hey Lil' Buddy! C'mon, this is going to be fun!"

Moby has never been the sharpest tool in the shed. In fact he's a bit of a blockhead. But even he knew something was up. He was hesitant to emerge, wondering why I had left the balls in the car. When I tugged at his collar, he pulled back, causing all his neck flub to bunch up around his face.

Finally, Moby noticed that the air outside the minivan was a veritable cornucopia of intriguing odors, so he jumped out to investigate. There were years' worth of animal pheromones, territorial markings, and nervous involuntary spillage in that parking lot. On my way to the clinic door, the leash stopped with a jolt while Moby sniffed, then licked, then marked a tuft of dead grass peeking through a crack in the asphalt. *Let him have his fun, poor guy.*

In the waiting room, Moby wasn't sure if he should hide or jump for joy. On one hand, there were lots of fun-looking dogs and people in there, and even one small hissy thing that made a peculiar yowling sound. (Moby had never seen a cat before.) But on the other hand, there were unfamiliar smells in that waiting room, like medicine...disinfectant...and fear.

Before Moby's blockhead could figure it all out, the veterinarian's assistant led him away. I watched his tail wag as he looked up at her, probably thinking he was going somewhere to chase balls. *Oh, the irony.*

Several hours later, Moby was back in the minivan, stunned at having been robbed of his virility and wondering why there was a ridiculous cone around his head.

The physical pain in his nether regions was a mere annoyance compared to the humiliation of the cone. It soon became the bane of his existence. He knocked over lamps and spilled his water. Worst of all, it got in the way of chasing balls.

At the end of the week, when Moby had accepted the fact he would be wearing that blasted cone for the rest of his life, it suddenly cracked and fell off while he was rolling in the snow. Moby stared at the cone a moment, not sure if he should be sad at losing another appendage or happy to be rid of it. Instinct took over, and Moby pounced onto the cone, grabbing and shaking it with all his might.

Killing the cone restored Moby's faith in his lingering masculinity, and as he trotted back to the house with his head held high, I could almost hear him say, "Nothing will ever get between me and my balls again."

SEASON 4 ◆ EPISODE 18

WHAT REMAINS TO BE SEEN

What happens when two parents, three kids, one overactive puppy, and several marauding mice are cooped up in a remote cabin in Maine, with no internet, no phone service, and no cable television during the last week of summer vacation?

The answer to my question depends on who's answering.

Hayden, despite the fact he was an opinionated college kid who loved nothing more than debating the palatability of dorm food or the effect of computerization on the global economy with his roommates, would have given the same response he had given to every parental question: "Good."

Anna, who relentlessly milked her victimization as the middle child, would claim that our end-of-summer vacation in Maine was like teetering on the precipice of hell.

Lilly would give a sincere response based on her genuine observations and honest opinions—right after she answered the five hundred and thirty-seven texts and social media posts she missed while we were off the grid.

Moby, in dog language, would say, "I loved it! I love you! I love my family! I love the cabin, the trees, the birds, the bugs, the sticks, the lake, the canoe, the lodge, the fire pit, the dirt!" Moby would blather on and on ad nauseam, until someone threw a ball or shook the dog food bag to distract him.

Ask Francis while we were stuck in two hours of Boston traffic on our way home, and he would've snapped impatiently at the kids to knock off the racket, complained his sciatica was killing him, and shouted in a hangry rage, "For the love of God could someone please get me a flipping snack from the cooler before I starve to death here?!"

Ask my otherwise pragmatic, rational husband the same question after we were back at home with the car unpacked and three pizza slices in his stomach, and he would offer a simple answer uncluttered by over-analysis and untainted with emotion—although possibly intended to shut me up—"It was a perfect vacation, Dear."

But what about my opinion? Was our family's week in the woods a success? Did we accomplish what we set out to do?

Did we pluck ourselves from the suffocating tidal wave of modern technology and rapidly changing cultural norms long enough to breathe in the fortifying strength of familial bonds and renew our uniquely human ties with the natural world?

Heck if I know.

I had to accept that it might take years before hindsight would bring the answers to my parenting questions into focus. In the meantime, I'd stop trying to draw conclusions and concentrate on making good memories.

Like everyone eating a late breakfast of hot buttered pancakes with peach slices, pecans, and Maine maple syrup. Like teaching Moby to swim. Like seeing my computer scientist son paddle around in a kayak. Like hiking Acadia trails in the rain. Like taking the whole family out in a canoe to watch the sun go down over the lake. Like being so bored on the fourth night in the cabin that, after watching our two-hour and five-minute DVD of *Dog Day Afternoon*, we watched it all over again with the director's commentary. Like hearing our girls giggling up in the loft after carving "I have lice" into the ceiling over their bunks. Like sipping local pale ale in Adirondack chairs around a roaring fire. Like beating Francis at Othello.

Like falling asleep to the scratching of mice and the call of the loons.

SEASON FIVE

ARE WE
THERE YET?

SEASON 5 ◆ EPISODE 1

LOST ON MEMORY LANE

I lifted the heavy wooden hatch over the narrow staircase leading to the basement. All the houses in our row of 120-year-old base quarters had hatches covering up the basement stairs. Each house in the row was like the other, but our house, Quarters C, had the scariest basement by far.

When the housing manager gave us the initial tour before we moved in, he took us down to the basement, a labyrinth of small spaces partitioned by studs half-covered by tacked-up pieces of drywall, stacked stone, and rickety cabinets from the turn of the century—not the most recent century, either. He was jittery as he led me into each space, flipping light switches as he went.

Strangely, he passed by one door as if it wasn't there. I stopped, grabbed the doorknob, and said, "What's this?" as I pushed the door inward. He scurried toward me.

"Oh, well, wait…" he bumbled nervously as I flipped the switch inside the door—and gasped.

A single lightbulb barely illuminated the large space, which I judged was under our living room. The floor was uneven dirt and rubble that rose up on one side toward a huge chunk of bedrock the house had been built over. The monstrous mound of rock was almost as tall as I was. It looked as though two eyes and a mouth might open to reveal Jabba the Hutt. Maybe the builders, unable to get rid of the outcropping of rock, decided to enclose it. Behind a door.

In the corner, a filthy dehumidifier hummed and rattled. The manager forced a shaky grin, advising me to keep that door closed. And so, I did.

But we used the other spaces of our scary basement to store our over-abundant belongings. My family often complains about my propensity to save everything from hospital bracelets to matchbooks, organized and categorized into bins in our basement. It's true, I've always felt compelled to squirrel things away, like my old Holly Hobbie sewing machine, Anna's and Lilly's confirmation dresses, Hayden's sock puppet, and the collar from our long-dead runt of a cat Zuzu.

When Hayden graduated from high school, I sent thirty-six t-shirts I'd been saving in a tub since he was a baby—from Montessori preschool, Taekwando, Boy Scouts, football, band—off to a quilter who made him a one-of-a-kind bedspread to memorialize his childhood. The quilt was such a meaningful graduation gift, I knew my hoarding tendencies were finally justified.

When Anna's graduation approached, I had to brave the basement labyrinth to find my stash of her t-shirts. With the heavy hatch secured to the wall, I descended the grey-painted stairs to our subterranean, cobwebbed, perpetually damp storage room. Normally, the fear in my gut would compel me to finish my task in the basement quickly and get back to the first floor. But on this day, what should have taken ten minutes took an entire afternoon and a half box of tissues.

The first tub I opened was full of baby items I hadn't seen in years. I let out a sigh and thought back more than a decade to those sweet moments when Anna was small enough to carry. There, in a musty fluorescent-lit corner, I got lost in memories. I caressed the soft flannel receiving blankets, remembering when she was born in a village hospital in England with an Irish midwife, who insisted I labor in a tub laced with lavender oil as she brought me tea and toast.

Pastel afghans, a tiny gingham dress, and Anna's baptismal cloth took me further away. The layers in the storage tub were like the rings of a tree. In between were lumps—a special rattle, a tattered pink doll, and a string of brightly-painted wooden beads. My eyes lost focus as I recalled Anna as a sleepy toddler, rhythmically stroking the beads, over and over.

The next box I found was full of old toys. I envisioned the plastic yellow baton, gripped in Anna's perpetually sticky fingers, relentlessly beating her chunky Fisher-Price xylophone. The purple cloth play purse took me back to our old house in Virginia, where Anna would strut around with the bag over one arm, stopping to apply the fake lipstick and pose precociously before a mirror.

Pink and yellow plates, cups, and pots looked exactly like they did when Anna served up smorgasbords of plastic toy pizza slices, hamburgers, peas, bananas, cupcakes, and cheese wedges. "Mmmm," I would say, smacking my lips loudly and pretending to chew, eliciting her brightly dimpled smile.

At the bottom of the box, a doll marked by an ink scribble in the middle of her forehead looked serenely relieved to have retired to a cardboard haven. Her life with Anna had not been easy. With the doll slumped in an umbrella stroller, Anna would push her around our cul-de-sac, sometimes hitting a crack that would catapult the poor doll head-first into the pavement. A quick kiss on the scuffed head, and Anna was off again.

A tattered file box contained artwork, crafts, and primitive pottery—ancient relics with cracking macaroni and yellowing glue. Strangely, these gave no indication of Anna's later talent for art and design. Small spiral notebooks were scribbled with her endless ideas, garment sketches, and redecorating plans. "How to make money this summer: 1. Sell my old Barbies; 2. Make lemonade; 3. ...," on one page. "Rules for Secret Club House," on another.

It's an incredible privilege to watch a human being grow, I thought. Cradling a helpless budding newborn in my arms, I couldn't have imagined the distinctive person who would bloom before my eyes over eighteen years.

I finally found the box of t-shirts, and the wonder of our exceptional daughter came into watery focus. Bossy, stubborn, controlling, and pensive. Intelligent, driven, hilarious, and creative. With big brown eyes, a sparkling smile, and an uncommon dimpled chin.

As I switched out the lights and lugged the box past the door to the lair of Jabba the Hutt, I realized I hadn't kept all those boxed relics for my children's sake. I had kept them for my sake, so I could remember. I squirreled items away that would take me back to the moments of motherhood I was afraid I'd forget.

Sniffling up the narrow stairs into the comforting afternoon light of my sunny kitchen, I shrugged off my irrational fear of losing childhood memories. Anna's high school graduation, like so many moments of her life, would surely be unforgettable. The monumental event would meld her past and present together, imprinting the incredible image of our daughter's evolution on my mind—forever.

SEASON 5 ◆ EPISODE 2

NEVER SAY NEVER

I swore I'd never do it.

But there I was on a gurney, begging my doctor to please, for the love of God, give me a flipping epidural right this minute. It was the birth of our third child, Lilly, and up until that point, I had insisted on enduring labor pains without medication.

Ridiculous, I know. Something a crunchy California nurse had said during my first prenatal classes had me believing epidurals caused prolonged contractions and emergency C-sections. However, twelve hours into labor number three, I discarded my fears, scruples, and dignity, and begged the doctor to inject me with something—morphine, vodka, battery acid, anything to stop the pain.

Life is funny like that. One minute, we think we have it all figured out, and the next thing we know, we've changed our own rules. Milestones like marriage, childbirth, military service, parenting teens, and financial responsibility present us with new sets of circumstances requiring new standards.

Before marriage, I rolled my eyes at those couples I'd see canoodling in public. "They're faking it," I thought, and believed people in real relationships didn't give each other eyelash kisses and lick ice cream off each other's noses. I thought I'd never be corny like them.

But then I met Francis.

Within weeks, we became one of those annoying couples who couldn't be in each other's presence without fingers laced or limbs intertwined. We would stare into each other's eyes, sniff each other's hair (Francis had hair in those days), and pick little bits of lint and crumbs off each other's clothing.

Nauseating!

During pregnancy, I said I would never nurse my baby in public, change his diaper while in an airplane seat, let him cry it out, strap him to a toddler leash, let him watch two Disney movies in a row, give his binky back after he dropped it in the dirt, or scream like a lunatic at his pee-wee soccer games.

Oh well.

Military spouses make rules to stay organized and deal with stress. Some proclaim they'll never live on base, join spouse clubs, or let the kids eat Fruit Loops for dinner during deployments. But at some point, "I will never" turns into "Don't knock it till you try it."

Parenting teenagers crushed my "never" edicts like walnuts. Despite my many prohibitions, I eventually gave in and let them use electronics in their rooms, watch R-rated movies, and wear jeans to church. And I'll admit—I've used my cell phone to call them for dinner, even when they're in the same house.

Once we felt the pinch of college tuition bills, I started pushing my Aldi cart a half mile across the parking lot in a torrential downpour just to get my quarter back. I've waited around at the commissary for a rotisserie chicken to be reduced to three ninety-nine. And after going to the movies (using a military discount) I've even found popcorn in my bra and eaten it.

Reality has driven us to do things we previously thought tacky, lazy, or negligent. But life's challenges and milestones have also revealed courage, strength, and character we never thought we had.

So, whether choosing between a minivan or a sports car, or deciding whether or not to stay in the military for twenty years, experience instills this simple life lesson: Never say never.

SEASON 5 ◆ EPISODE 3

ONCE A MILITARY FAMILY

It was seven in the morning, and the late summer sun was already shining crisp and bright on the train platform. Francis hastily parked my luggage at my feet, inadvertently nicking my toe in the process.

"Oooh, sorry Hon, but I'd better get to work. Call me when you get to your mother's." He leaned down to give me a quick kiss goodbye. He was wearing his khaki uniform—buttoned, tucked, pinned, and polished. As a navy wife, I've become quite accustomed to goodbyes, but this one felt different.

I observed the other passengers waiting and drew conclusions about their lives. A sleepy student, a hip grandmother, an arrogant businessman. It dawned on me they had taken notice of Francis's uniform, and deduced: A military family.

The uniform I often took for granted had defined us for more than two decades.

The uniform symbolized not only Francis's military service, but mine as a military spouse and our kids' as military brats. It told a tale of duty, deployments, separation, transition, challenges, hardships, patriotism, pride, and adventure. The uniform spoke to the strength, resiliency, and courage of the people who wore it, washed it, and hung it on the backs of their kitchen doors.

At our wedding in 1993, Francis was a young navy lieutenant

and I was a brand-new attorney. Within two years, we rocked our baby boy, Hayden, in base quarters in Monterey, California, at the Naval Postgraduate School. In another couple years, we were in rural England, where Anna was born by an Irish midwife, and where Francis drove a beat-up Fiat on dark, winding roads to stand the watch. A few years later, we were in Virginia Beach, where Francis completed a sea tour, three shore tours, and a yearlong deployment to Djibouti while our family grew to include our youngest daughter, Lillian.

After a three-year adventure in Stuttgart, Germany, we found ourselves at Naval Station Mayport, Florida, where we could see dolphins, frigates, and destroyers in the Atlantic waves just outside our base house's kitchen window. Then, in Rhode Island at the U.S. Naval War College, in the twilight of a long military career, we watched our children use their skills as military kids to succeed in high school and college.

A rooster suddenly crowed from behind a house across the tracks, bringing me back to the train platform. I gulped hard, remembering that in a few short months, Francis would retire from the military.

Where do we go from here? I wondered, squinting at the sun's reflection on the tracks. Francis and his uniform were long gone, and I was there, just another passenger on the crowded platform. *Is this what it's like in the civilian world?*

"Stand clear of the yellow line, fast train approaching," blared a voice from the loudspeakers. Instinctively, I gripped my heart, as a flash of metal and momentum blew by, sucking the air from my chest and clearing the cache of my wandering mind.

Our military identity lay deep within our hearts, not in outward signs and symbols. Even with Francis's uniform stored in the back of the hall closet, he would always be a navy veteran. And our family would always be a military family, through and through.

The Number 95 arrived right on time, and as I stepped off the platform and onto the train, I knew our military life was not coming to an end. We were simply boarding the next train on our journey.

SEASON 5 ◆ EPISODE 4

SHOP, DROP, AND ENROLL

"Three decorative pillows or just two?" Anna asked in front of a colorful display of bedding at a local store. It was seven in the evening, and we had been shopping since the stores opened that morning.

The first place we stopped was the Apple Store, where I spent more than a thousand bucks in less than fifteen minutes buying Anna a new laptop that was required for her major. After that we hit Zara, H&M, Macy's, JCPenney, Target, Walmart, Bed Bath & Beyond, Joann Fabrics, T.J.Maxx, and HomeGoods.

"What's another twenty bucks at this point?" I replied to Anna in utter defeat and near starvation. "Definitely get three."

Two weeks later, Francis, Anna, and I pulled up to her dorm at Syracuse University, our minivan packed to the gills with fluffy new bedding, posters, a clip-on lamp, school supplies, throw rug, shower caddy, towels, desk set, fan, pop-up laundry bins, six months' worth of toiletries, various snacks, cases of bottled water, a microwave, a coffee maker, and yes, three decorative pillows.

Happy, helpful sophomores garbed in blazing orange, whose parents had been victims of "The Dorm Room Shakedown" the previous year, were awaiting our arrival with huge rolling bins to cart thousands of dollars' worth of unnecessary products up to assigned rooms.

"Hi!" they shouted with rehearsed enthusiasm, shaking us out of our road trip stupor, "I'm Sean/Cassandra/Matt! I'd love to help you move in!" They filled two of the rolling carts to capacity, then guided us like sheep to the dorm elevators.

In the newfangled coed hallway, Anna found her room, which was a "split double"—one room separated down the middle by a wall of closets and dressers. This gave Anna and her roommate their own private spaces within one room.

Anna's roommate, Chandler, had already moved in, and her side was spectacular. It looked like something straight out of a Pottery Barn catalog. We stared at her shabby chic bedside table, complete with a vase of peonies and a trendy mirrored lamp. There were whitewashed faux ironwork wall hangings, cool enlarged letters, clear canisters filled whimsically with popcorn and pretzels. Her rug was larger, her bed risers were higher, and she had way more than three decorative pillows.

Concerned that Anna's room would look like a cell at Rikers Island by comparison, we quickly unloaded everything we'd already purchased, and left to find the nearest Target. Another two hundred bucks later, we added modern shelving, storage bins, two strings of twinkle lights, curtains, a coat rack, hangers, plastic drawers, and a bowl of fresh fruit.

While Anna and I scrambled to decorate, Francis retreated to the busy coed hallway. "Eyes forward!" we heard him bark in military fashion when passing boys tried to sneak a peek at his daughter.

Before saying goodbye to Anna the next day, we all went to her dining hall to take advantage of the free lunch offered to new parents. I contemplated filling my purse with chicken tenders to supplement the beans and rice we'd be eating at home for the next six months but selected a modest plateful of quinoa-spinach-mango salad and coconut shrimp instead.

"You know, Anna," Francis said between mouthfuls of made-to-order chicken salad panini, "when I went to college, all I brought was the blue quilt off my bed and a Journey poster. And our dining hall only had things like casseroles and meatloaf. Do you have any idea how lucky you are?"

Looking confused, Anna chomped her gourmet veggie pizza and said, "Want anything from the fro-yo bar?"

When it was all said and done, Anna's room looked better than the hotel room we stayed in at the Syracuse Holiday Inn and had much better coffee. But then again, our hotel was only a hundred bucks with our military discount. I guess the old adage is true: You get what you pay for.

Or in this case, your college kids get what you pay for.

SEASON 5 ◆ EPISODE 5

FOR THE ONES LEFT BEHIND

I was entering the tenth grade when I suddenly became the object of my parents' undivided attention. It seemed as though their eyes were locked on me, reading my every thought, prying at my secrets, peering uninvited into my soul.

The light over the dinner table swayed, uncomfortably bright. Beads of cold sweat dotted my hairline. Every night, I braced myself for the inevitable interrogation....

"How do you like the roast, Dumpling?" Mom asked, with a nonchalance that belied her intrusive stare.

"Delicious, Mom," I sputtered between cheekfulls of beef and potatoes, hoping the compliment might end my ordeal.

"So, what happened at school today?" my father pressed while pushing applesauce around his plate.

Wide-eyed and hunched in a self-protective posture at the opposite end of our kitchen table, I muttered the one word that had allowed me to avoid my parents' attention for so many years: "Nothin'."

"Well, *something* must've happened at school today. Here, I'll help you out. So...you stepped off the bus, and *then*?" he badgered, mercilessly. So it went, night after night.

My brother, Tray, had gone off to the U.S. Naval Academy, leaving me at home, alone with my parents. For so many years, I had flown completely under the radar. But now, my only sibling was gone.

As the first born, Tray had always carried the entire burden of my parents' expectations for their offspring. I had been merely the unremarkable little sister of The Golden Boy, The Favorite, The Apple of Their Eye. Tray not only fulfilled but exceeded their hopes—he was a popular top athlete with gifted math and science skills who went on to become a navy jet pilot. His obvious superiority left me free to drift contentedly through childhood, bouncing unnoticed between mediocre and above average.

Wearing ratty Converse Chucks, hand-me-down jean cut-offs, and a camp t-shirt, I'd ride my yellow Schwinn through our neighborhood, my Kool-Aid backpack packed with a cheese sandwich, a few Wacky Package collector's cards, and a Thermos of Tang. On rainy days I'd stay in my room, lost in elaborate pretend scenarios, or I'd play my mother's old forty-fives on my Fisher-Price record player.

As a child, I did not resent Tray for getting all my parents' attention. Quite the contrary, I relished my quiet, comfortable, ignored existence, and happily hid in the humongous shadow of the older brother I idolized.

But then he left home, and the jig was up.

It was as if my parents, Durwood and Diane, looked through the unexpected void left by my brother's absence and noticed, "Oh yeah...Who is that there? Is that the other one...what's her name again? Oh yes! It's Lisa!"

Mom was now interested in what I wore, my social behavior, and how I did my hair. "Oh, Dumpling, let me help you give a little height to those bangs," she would say, licking her thumb.

My dad, who had no previous interest in my athletic accomplishments, which by the way included a second-place ribbon for the standing broad jump at church camp, started showing up to all my high school swim meets. My teammates knew this sudden change in attention made me nervous and would alert me when he appeared in the chlorine-steamed stands, "Heads up, Lisa! Durwood's here!"

Night after agonizing night, I was interrogated by my parents at the dinner table, forced to reveal my likes, dislikes, social pursuits, academic achievements, ambitions, disappointments, hopes, and dreams. Durwood and Diane took an unprecedented interest in me, having long talks about life, getting me horseback riding lessons, taking photographs of me before dances, and bragging about me to their friends.

It was like I was their kid or something. *Weird.*

Decades later, our youngest child, Lilly, sat wide-eyed and defensively crouched in her chair at the dinner table, as if we were about to pummel her with dinner rolls. Hayden had been away at college for a couple of years, and Anna had left for college the week before. Lilly's instinct was telling her, the jig is up.

But I let Lilly know, there's nothing to fear. I'd lived through it myself and was there to tell the tale about how those left behind suddenly become the center of attention.

The strange people who ignored you all these years? Don't worry, Lilly, they won't hurt you. They are simply your parents, and they've finally realized you are pretty darned interesting after all.

SEASON 5 ◆ EPISODE 6

THE ELEPHANT IN
THE BEDROOM

I'd seen those awkward commercials. Unrealistically tall, thin, good-looking actors holding hands in outdoor bathtubs and canoodling in public. The woman had silky long hair and flowing garments that looked like they might fall off at the slightest tug, and the man had a rugged jawline, piercing blue eyes, and impossibly white teeth. They exchanged come-hither stares and knowing smiles, as one led the other by the hand toward the bedroom....

But I'd been married a long time. I knew igniting passion was not a matter of popping a little blue pill. Presumably, Francis had plenty of lead in his pencil. It was the numerous *other* realities of everyday married life that got in the way of romance.

On any given night, Francis and I started yawning—not a particularly attractive human reflex I might add—about an hour after dinner, the sure sign that we only had one crime show in us before our eyelids would drop. My yawns began discreetly, but as I reached maximum inhale, my face contorted, my nostrils flared and my double chin tripled. Francis, on the other hand, made a dramatic scene of every yawn, with a gasping deep inhale, followed by a hacking exhale that made everyone around him duck for cover, and ending with a bizarre jaw-chattering finish that sounded something like, "Gi-gi-gi-gi-gi-gahhh!"

When we finally trudged upstairs to our bedroom, we didn't just hop in the sack. As a middle-aged couple with achy joints, breathing issues, and persnickety bedtime habits, there was a whole rigmarole we still had to go through before we could actually attempt sleep.

Unfortunately, this routine was not conducive to romance.

After the dog, Moby, dutifully flopped into his crate in our bedroom, Francis headed to the bathroom in his boxer shorts. With the door wide open, he made all necessary deposits before flushing and leaving the seat up. Then he stood at the mirror, trying to decide whether it was worth brushing his teeth or not. Groggy-eyed, we passed in the hallway just as Francis finished up an especially noisy yawn. "Aaaah (inhaling)...achhhhhh (the hacking exhale)...Gi, gi, gi, gi, gahhh (the dramatic finish)!"

After brushing and flossing, I took my fiber pills and ginkgo biloba, and then inserted the bulky, drool-producing mouth guard that kept me from grinding my teeth.

"I'm ex-*thauth-ted*," I announced with a night-guard lisp after entering the bedroom. I put on my flannel pjs, while Francis fiddled with the equipment on his nightstand. It took a few minutes for him to fix the complicated straps of his sleep apnea headgear, and at the same time, I wrestled with the Velcro fasteners of my plantar fasciitis night splint boot.

Francis flipped a switch, and I heard the whirr of his CPAP machine.

I placed an extra pillow under my knees to stave off hip pains and opened my book. Francis couldn't sleep with the lights on, so I grabbed the reading glasses I had recently found at a local discount store with little LED lights built into them. I pressed the buttons on either side of the lenses, and two piercing rays illuminated the pages of my book.

"Good night Thweetie," I lisped in the dark.

Francis jerked out of a half slumber, and like something out of *Alien*, turned his head toward me with four feet of flexible tubing extending from the rubber nose piece strapped to his face. I glanced over at him from my contour pillow, looking like some kind of drooling underground miner, and nearly blinded him with my laser beams.

He squinted in recognition and mumbled an airy reply through his plastic elephant trunk, "GNooo nihhht, Hhhonhhee."

A few minutes later, in the white noise silence of our marital bedroom, ironically, the dog began to snore.

I sighed and figured, any couple who manages to get in the mood in the midst of middle-aged reality has far more passion in their marriage than any little blue pill could ever provide.

SEASON 5 ◆ EPISODE 7

TRAVELING ON AUTO POTTY

It was June, time for my annual columnists' conference. The events were held in different cities each year, and I looked forward to getting away from my "home office" (i.e., my laptop on the kitchen table) flying off to a different location and feeling like a real journalist.

This time, I was headed all the way to Los Angeles to spend a long weekend with the group of newspaper columnists that had become both professional colleagues and friends since I joined the group in 2010.

In all the years of military moves and traveling, I never loved flying, but I felt a certain excitement that day about going off on my own away from Francis and the kids and the perpetually repeating responsibilities of being a wife and mother. After a quick goodbye with Francis at curb-side drop off, I wheeled my bag confidently into the Providence airport, chin in the air, pre-printed boarding pass in hand, heels clicking—playing the part of a seasoned traveling professional.

Damn, security screening. The hassle of flying always took me by surprise.

My role as a traveling journalist shriveled as I entered the raw humanity of the TSA line. I shuffled forward, foot by foot, staring clumsily at the same twenty people every time we zigzagged past each other toward the security screening agents who held our destinies in their latex-gloved hands. Thirty minutes later, I'd formed a silent kinship with my fellow travelers. In the microcosm of airport society, they were my friends. At the end of the line, I bid them a temporary adieu and nervously approached the TSA agent's podium.

The agent looked from my documentation to my face to my ID, making me feel like a fugitive wanted for heinous crimes. I feared that TSA German shepherds might sense my natural guilt complex and attack, but somehow I passed and was directed to the security screening conveyor belts.

Everyone tried to act nonchalant as we fumbled for grey plastic bins. We wanted to appear to be a savvy travelers, but all were uneasy with the indignity of the process. I scrambled to remember the complicated rules: Do I remove my jacket in addition to my shoes and belt? If my laptop has to be in a bin by itself, does my phone get its own bin too? Will that packet of ketchup in my purse be flagged as liquid? Will the screener think my hairdryer is a gun?

I stood, legs spread and arms over my head, in the futuristic metal detector as an exhaled puff blew my hair into the air. The lady behind me was selected for a random pat-down. I tried not to gawk. We retrieved our bins, and as my comrades and I put our shoes and belts back on, I felt like we'd all had an awkward one-night stand.

Finally headed toward my gate, I stopped to get a cup of coffee, but the Dunkin' Donuts line was longer than the one at TSA. Turned out, I had plenty of time. My flight was delayed two hours due to a flight attendant calling in sick at the last minute.

The large latte hit my bladder about a half hour before boarding, so I went in search of restrooms. Heeding the prohibition against leaving bags unattended, I muscled my wheeled carry-on into one of the many stalls, latched the door, straddled the humongous bag, and grabbed for the paper seat cover dispenser. The first three paper covers ripped in half, the fourth fell into the toilet while I was trying to position it, and the fifth one disappeared when the toilet unexpectedly flushed. Those phantom flushes in automatic public toilets had always scared the you-know-what out of me, which ironically would have defeated the entire purpose of being in the toilet in the first place.

With a seat cover finally in place, I took my position.

Strangely, the otherwise noisy bathroom fell dead silent. I could see the feet of the occupants next to me, but I heard only silence. I hoped someone would turn on the sink, while my bladder refused to release the sixty-four ounces of coffee I'd consumed that morning.

I had experienced bathroom stage fright on other occasions, most notably in college when perpetually clogged bar toilets caused long lines in the bathrooms. The one working toilet usually had no toilet paper, a broken door lock, and gaps in the stall that allowed everyone in line to stare through the cracks. Once it was my turn to go, I was paralyzed.

While waiting there with my elbows on my knees, it occurred to me that travel pottying had changed significantly since I was a kid. On family trips, my dad would pull over our station wagon to the side of the road for quick pit stops. If we managed to find a gas station with a bathroom, it wasn't worth the effort because Maz insisted on spreading half a roll of toilet paper on the seat before I was allowed to sit down. Francis had told me his family didn't even bother to stop, because they kept a large mayonnaise container known as the "tinkle jar" in the back window of their station wagon.

But those improvised methods of yesteryear were no longer considered apropos—or sanitary for that matter. I sat there in that state-of-the-art public toilet facility, unable to go, longing for the simple practicality of a roadside patch of weeds.

At one point, I fidgeted, and—WHOOSH!—set off the phantom flusher again. It scared the bejeezus out of me—and provided the nudge my bladder needed. Relief!

The toilet paper was affixed to some type of conservation dispenser that stopped the roll at each half turn. The flimsy tissue ripped with the slightest resistance, forcing me to make several attempts—roll, stop, rip, roll, stop, rip, roll, stop, rip—until I had enough scraps to do the job.

Finally, I got up to trigger the flusher, which up until now had seemed able to react to a falling eyelash from three stalls down. However, nothing happened. I stood there, wondering if the sensor had a tiny camera inside that transmitted to a flushing control room. Had the person on duty gone to lunch? I swiveled my hips, bobbed my head, and waved my hands to no avail.

With only minutes to boarding, I gave up on flushing and left the stall. Halfway to the sinks, I heard it—WHOOSH! I imagined the flushing controller giggling over his ham and cheese.

The bank of sinks had no knobs, controls, or buttons. "Here we go again," I thought, waving my hands in search of automated soap and water. I had a choice of hand dryers: a high-tech version powerful enough to take off my skin, or the old-fashioned kind that emits a warm breeze and eventually ends with me giving up and wiping my hands on my pants.

Frustrated with newfangled automation, I chose the latter.

Soon after takeoff, the flight attendant came by.

"Coffee?" he asked.

"Sure," I said, secretly wondering if anyone had an empty mayonnaise jar somewhere on the plane.

SEASON 5 ◆ EPISODE 8

THE HAIR OF THE DOG

I didn't believe those who warned us.

"You're getting a Labrador retriever?" they asked in disbelief. "You know Labs shed, right?"

Yeah, yeah. Whatever.

When I first set eyes on our puppy, Moby, he was eight weeks old and adorable. Someone could've said he would grow up to have poisonous tentacles, razor sharp claws, and skunk-like scent sacs. I simply wouldn't have cared. He looked just like one of those impossibly precious L.L.Bean catalog puppies, and nothing, including common sense, was going to stop me from taking him home.

Throughout the spring, our new dog shed a hair here and there, but we were too busy dealing with other puppy-related issues such as potty training and wound care from the playful nips of his needle-sharp teeth to notice.

Then summer came. Moby turned six months, and to celebrate his follicles apparently decided to retire. Accordingly, his stiff little yellow hairs were granted their freedom to explore every nook and cranny of our household.

It all happened quite suddenly. One day, to praise Moby for returning the pair of underwear he had stolen from Hayden's room, I reached down to stroke his back. He gave me several licks to the face before I noticed I had a veritable catcher's mitt of dog hair covering my hand.

Since then, dog hair has permeated every aspect of our lives.

First thing in the morning, my scratchy throat was the sure sign I'd inhaled several hairs in the middle of the night, triggering sudden coughing fits. When I shook the covers to make our bed, puffs of hair became airborne, creating a cyclone of dog hair that glowed visibly in the morning light, before gently drifting back down to settle on our bedspread, ready to be inhaled another night.

Hair floating in my morning coffee either got fished out with a finger or ended up on my tongue. Strangely, if it ended up in my mouth I could feel it, but somehow couldn't seem to find it. Eventually, I swallowed and hoped dog hair didn't have too many carbs.

For the rest of the day, I found mats of dog hair in the lint trap, tumbleweeds drifting down the hallway, tufts on the upholstery, balls on the bathroom rug, blankets in the vacuum filter, tangles on the fan blades, and a generous sprinkling of hair on carpets, furniture, and fixtures.

Also, thanks to my unfortunate mistake of allowing Moby to ride along in the minivan, anyone who entered our vehicle got out looking like Chewbacca.

I didn't think it was canine-ly possible for a dog to shed so much, much less for it to end up on top of our refrigerator, baked into the meatloaf, or woven into my toothbrush bristles.

In a strange and incredibly annoying sort of way, I thought, *dog shedding is quite miraculous.*

I knew it would be a miracle if I survived the process without hacking up a hairball myself. But in the meantime, I'd have no choice but to love every hair on—or off—Moby's adorable head.

SEASON 5 ◆ EPISODE 9

FOR PITY'S SAKE

Trailing tissues behind, I burst through the base clinic doors five minutes past my appointment time. "Sorry, I'm late," I croaked to the military medical corpsman at the family practice desk. He directed me to the waiting area.

Fishing another crumpled Kleenex from my pocket, I nestled in to read juicy gossip about *The Bachelor* from a dog-eared waiting room copy of *US* magazine, just as someone bellowed from behind me, "Lisa Molinari?"

Dang.

With my legs dangling like a child from the papered examining table, I waited patiently for the doctor's arrival, mulling over the possible outcomes.

With this terrible cough, sore throat, and congestion, it must be very serious. One listen to my chest and surely, she will prescribe antibiotics and steroid treatments. Hmm...she might very well diagnose pneumonia and order me to spend a week in the hospital under an oxygen tent, so I'd better think of someone who could stop by to walk the dog, I thought.

As I envisioned myself securely ensconced in sterile plastic while friends and family visited with chocolate milkshakes, Dr. Jenkins entered the room in a hurried swish.

"Hello, Mrs. Molinari. What brings you in today?"

I was always one of those people who believe all stories should be told properly. Even the tiniest detail could be essential in painting the right picture, conveying the correct tone, and maintaining complete accuracy.

"Well, Doc, it all started last Monday," I began. I told her all about how Francis has been gone, how tired I've been lately, that I may have picked up something at Lilly's high school which is a veritable petri dish by the way, that my to-do list is a mile long, etcetera, etcetera.

Much to my surprise, Dr. Jenkins didn't seem to be listening. As I was detailing the issues I'd been having with my minivan's steering, she asked with her back to me, "What color is your sputum?"

Answering that question required admitting to shamelessly inspecting the unmentionable globs I'd spit into a sink or blown into tissues. Everyone had done it, but couldn't the doctor just take my word for it that I was very sick? Assuming she needed another detailed explanation, I went on, "Well, let's see, I blew my nose in church on Sunday, and wasn't able to take a look until I got home, and—"

Halfway through explaining a particular shade of olive green, Dr. Jenkins turned around and came at me with a reflex hammer, repeatedly rapping at my face with the pointed end. "Does this hurt?" she asked between blows. For a split second, I pondered how one might answer such a stupid question.

Hell, yes! was just too obvious, and asking, *I don't know, does this hurt?* as I kicked her in the shin seemed too hostile, so I went for, "Is the Pope Catholic?"

By now I could tell that this doctor operated with the fundamental belief that all patients were hypochondriacs, wimps, and liars with nothing better to do than to spend hours in base clinics feigning illnesses, just so they could wait for more hours in the pharmacy for antibiotics they don't need, which would eventually result in the spread of antibiotic-resistant super-bugs that would soon infect and destroy all of mankind.

As I began to snort and suck at the back of my throat in an attempt to bring up or down some kind of concrete proof to make my case, Dr. Jenkins said, "Your chest sounds clear, so I'll treat you for viral bronchitis. Pump the fluids and Mucinex." She was gone in a swish.

I wondered if she'd question her Hippocratic oath when she discovered I had to be airlifted to the ER for intravenous antibiotics later that night.

No such luck. Five days later, the raspy voice, the sore throat, the barking cough, and the technicolor phlegm had all but disappeared. I had to admit, Dr. Jenkins was right. *Still*, I ruminated, *shouldn't doctors realize the proper treatment for moms who are alone and sick is sometimes simply a little sympathy?*

Chocolate milkshakes wouldn't hurt either.

SEASON 5 ◆ EPISODE 10

THE BOY IS BACK IN TOWN

There were times when we had to avoid a certain room in our creaky old house. I told people it was a dangerous hazard, a treacherous obstacle, a toxic wasteland, and advised those who entered to wear eye protection and use a gas mask.

Buried deep in debris and dirty gym socks was the creature who was responsible for turning that otherwise livable room into a veritable landfill every time he came home from college: our son, Hayden.

Every time Hayden left to go back to college, it took me a month to turn his bedroom into an acceptable guest room. It wasn't just a matter of cleaning—more like the disaster restoration services that trained professionals performed after fires, floods, or lethal mold infestations.

The room stayed clean until Hayden came home from college on break, and the cycle repeated itself all over again.

I had placed clean sheets on the bed and tidied the room before Hayden came home. But after a few days, the mattress was bare of linens, which were presumably thrown off in the middle of the night and lay crumpled in a dusty corner. The bed was strewn with gum wrappers, cords, empty soda cans, and wrinkled clothing. The floor was covered with piles of neglected books, tech boxes, tangled electronics, crusty dishes, and stiffened gym clothes.

Every flat surface held teetering stacks of college boy cast-offs, all coated in an unhealthy sprinkling of dust and toenail clippings.

Interestingly, none of this seemed to interfere with Hayden's routine while home on break. He was perfectly happy to wake up at noon on his litter-strewn mattress, wearing the same pizza sauce stained t-shirt he wore the day before, and stumble like a zombie with crazed hair down to the kitchen for his daily roast beef sandwich, which he liked to consume on the couch while watching old episodes of *Judge Judy*, wiping his hands on the upholstery.

After a sufficient number of crumbs had been deposited on the carpet, Hayden headed back to his bedroom, somehow negotiating the familiar piles of debris without so much as a scratch, to spend a few hours on one of several electronic devices before getting serious about his schedule.

Sometime in the mid-afternoon, he emerged once again from his personal cesspool, ready to face the day, or what was left of it, with vim and vigor. He had not yet shaved, combed his hair, or changed his clothes, but he managed to grab his coat (which doubled as a blanket while his bedding was in that forgotten corner) and his shoes (both of which remained untied).

He spent the rest of his day walking the dog, going to the gym, and visiting friends. I wondered if Hayden's buddies were alarmed by his disheveled state, but I soon realized young men his age were too caught up in youthful exuberance to care.

He returned home in time for dinner, during which he consumed his meal in a manner normally associated with ravenous wolverines. To his credit, Hayden courteously dropped his fork and plate into the dishwasher before retiring to his putrid quarters for the night. We reminded him to take a shower, which he always did, even if it occurred at 1:00 a.m., after phone calls to various friends, watching old movies, and playing a few rounds of *Pokémon Super Mystery Dungeon*.

We eventually took him back to college, after which I excavated, fumigated, and disinfected his room so guests could sleep there without breaking an ankle, being strangled by electrical cords, or contracting a fungal infection or Legionnaire's Disease.

Why did we enable our son to live in such a primitive and unsanitary way when he was home from college? Shouldn't we, a military family, have required him to wake with morning reveille and spend his day with productive, ship-shape pursuits?

Perhaps.

But knowing Hayden tackled differential equations, algorithms, and software design courses while at school, we figured he deserved every break he could get. Besides, we knew one day soon enough, our kids would all graduate from college and be out on their own. When that finally happened, our rooms would be perpetually clean and ready for guests—with gleaming surfaces, fresh linens, hospital corners, and the toilet paper folded into a triangle.

And then, we'd long for the days when our home was dirtier, because that was when it was our kids' home too.

SEASON 5 ◆ EPISODE 11

BOWL DAY: A PLAY-BY-PLAY

Football-shaped bowl of nuts was on the coffee table. Starter log was sputtering in the fireplace. Dog had been walked. Wings were in the oven.

Official play begins.

Francis, ensconced in his tattered college sweatshirt, cargo pants he bought himself off the sale rack at Target, and ratty old sheepskin slippers, surveyed the field, attempting to locate the best seating formation for maximum game-viewing comfort. Uncapped beer in hand, he glanced around to be sure I was not in the room, then hovered over my favorite spot on the couch.

Francis didn't utilize his quadriceps to gradually lower his weight into a seat like most human beings; instead, the instant he felt his knees break their upright locked position, he disengaged all muscles, allowing his entire torso to plummet toward his desired location. Interestingly, Francis, all three of his brothers, and their father were infamous chair wreckers, leaving snapped legs, warped springs, and crooked recliners in their wakes.

As if seized with temporary paralysis of his lower extremities, Francis's knees buckled, sending his girth rocketing toward our aging couch with violent impact.

GUH-GLUNK!

Unnecessary roughness.

Entering the room, I saw Hayden sitting on the floor munching from a bag of tortilla chips, and Francis in my seat. Hoping a bit of nagging would roust him, I harped, "Hey Hon, if you insist on watching the game from my favorite spot, could you at least sit down gently? Every time you sit there, I hear that spring clunk under you like it's broken or something."

"God help me," he grumbled under his breath.

I settled temporarily for the other end of our couch and realized Francis's offensive move required a smarter defense. "You know, I think you'd better poke that fire Honey, you know how unpredictable those starter logs can be."

Francis looked at me suspiciously, but I feigned ignorance, "Have the Seahawks' colors changed? Didn't they have royal-blue jerseys a few years ago?"

As Francis stepped toward the fireplace, I inconspicuously employed a slide-lift-blitz maneuver to regain my territory. But just as I reached the center cushion, our dog, Moby, appeared, licking my face.

Interference.

GUH-GLUNK!

"Alright guys, c'mon, let's get some real points on the board!" Francis yelled after swiftly retaking *my* rightful seat. To add insult to injury, he lobbed his ratty sheepskin-slippered foot into my lap and slurped the last of his beer.

Unsportsmanlike conduct.

"Hey, Mom?"

"Yes," I muttered, after unclenching my teeth.

"Are those wings done yet?"

"Not yet," I looked over just as Hayden tipped the bag of chips above his open mouth, triggering a mini-avalanche of corner crumbs, which cascaded into his mouth, eyes, shirt, and the freshly-vacuumed family room carpet, "But I'm fairly certain you'll survive."

Just then, the cells of my brain called a huddle—a new play was forming.

Time out.

While Francis and Hayden laughed like simpletons at silly beer commercials, I disappeared into the kitchen, returning a few minutes later with a heaping tray of hot wings. Like a dedicated wife and mother, I smilingly doled out platefuls to my unsuspecting husband and son.

And then I waited, nibbling patiently on a stalk of celery.

As expected, they dug right in, Hayden meticulously dissecting each tiny radius, ulna, and humerus, then sucking each finger from base to tip. Francis, on the other hand, plopped whole wings into his open mouth, and after manipulation with teeth and tongue, pulled the bones out from his pursed lips, stripped clean of meat, fat, skin and cartilage.

"Whew!" Francis exclaimed, wiping his brow with a sauce-stained napkin, "Spicy, huh?!"

Hayden was the first casualty, running for a soda, while Francis tenaciously sweated through another wing or two before abandoning his position in search of cold beer to soothe his burning lips.

Thanks to a few extra shakes of hot sauce, my play had worked. With the coast finally clear, I mustered what was left of my middle-aged agility.

Hail Mary.

Reentering the room, Francis saw me, firmly seated in my favorite spot on our couch. I pumped my upturned hands in the air while wiggling my knees back and forth, in a victory dance.

Score.

SEASON 5 ◆ EPISODE 12

FIFTY SHADES OF MATTRESS SHOPPING

I stepped out of our car and squinted up at the sleek, tall building. It seemed more like a tech company or a global banking institution or the corporate headquarters of something really important.

Not a furniture store.

Francis and I hiked across what seemed like acres of parking lot toward the enormous entrance with its gliding automatic doors and gleaming blue Cardi's Furniture sign. We stopped inside and stared, mouths agape, at the massive lobby before us.

The ceiling soared five stories overhead. Outdoor furniture was everywhere—wicker, teak, canvas, and cotton stripe. Ahead, crisscrossing escalators chugged hordes of shoppers up and down to floors filled with furniture displays.

"How can I help you?" a salesman asked, appearing out of nowhere. He was balding, wore an open-collared lilac shirt, a silver pinky ring, and grey slacks. I avoid hard-sales pitches, but Francis can't resist the opportunity to have someone's undivided attention. He widened his stance, crossed his arms, and began.

"Thanks for your help, uh," he squinted at the name tag on the man's lilac shirt, "Joe. My name is Francis, and I just retired after twenty-eight years in the navy. My wife Lisa and I are…"

"Well, thank you for your service," Joe schmoozed, glancing at both of us.

"I appreciate that, Joe. Truthfully, it was my honor. When I showed up for Aviation Officer Candidate School down in Pensacola back in 1988, I never imagined that I'd end up making military service a career. But I've enjoyed every minute of it. Even my last deployment to..."

"Joe," I interrupted, "do you have mattresses?"

Francis took the hint and fast-forwarded his life story to the end. "Our last military move is next month, Joe, and we need a new bed."

"Right this way," Joe said. He led us to the elevator doors and said, "Press three."

The third floor displayed mattresses as far as the eye could see. We didn't know where to begin. For the first half of our marriage, we used low-budget mattresses from the military exchange. Then, in 2011, we found a Sears clearance center in Jacksonville, Florida, where we bought a slightly scuffed, queen-sized pillow-top that was leaning against a wall between a scratch-and-dent refrigerator and a reconditioned lawn mower.

Classy.

"How can I help you today?" Another salesman appeared magically. This one was named Pete. He had comb-lines in his hair and wore an open-collared blue shirt, a gold pinky ring, and black slacks. Francis widened his stance and squinted at Pete's name tag.

Here we go again.

After Francis finished his life story, Pete led us through the sea of quilted polyester. Like Vanna White, he motioned for us to lie down on the first luxurious king-sized bed.

"Which side do you prefer?" he asked me. It seemed odd, exposing my bedtime preferences to a complete stranger, but I took the left side, and Francis flopped onto the right, groaning loudly with pleasure.

"Oh, yeah, Pete, that's what I'm talking about!"

Pete showed us three more models, each time hovering over us, asking intimate questions. "Do you move around a lot? Do you get sweaty? Do you like to have your legs raised? Do you prefer soft or firm?"

I felt cheap and violated, but I noticed other couples testing mattresses too—bouncing around, spooning, and flopping from side to side. I decided I was being silly, and finally surrendered to the process.

Mind over mattress, I told myself.

"I like this one," I announced, "so how much does it cost?"

Pete gestured to a felt flap over the end of the bed. Like Vanna revealing the Wheel of Fortune Bonus Puzzle, he flipped the cover to reveal the price.

I nearly choked on my uvula.

Pete tried to snap us out of our sticker shock by offering sixty-month no-interest financing. *This weekend only, of course.* When this didn't work, he led us directly to the economy section, where we spooned and flopped until we found a decent mattress in our price range.

In other words, we slept our way to the bottom.

SEASON 5 ◆ EPISODE 13

THE TRUTH ABOUT OUR SON

"It's a boy," Doc Walker had said as calmly as if he'd said, "Please pass the salt." It was April 4, 1995, at the hospital in Monterey, California. After twelve hours of labor turned the whites of my eyes blood red, I eagerly grasped the waxy, bluish, nine-pound baby boy we named Hayden.

Two weeks later, when Hayden wouldn't stop crying and refused to feed, I called the pediatrician. Hayden had just smiled at us for the first time that morning. But my instincts told me something was wrong.

The pediatrician met us at his office, even though it was after hours—no messing around when newborns are concerned. As soon as he saw the mottled color of Hayden's skin, he ordered us to go directly to the emergency room. After a hurried spinal tap, his suspicions were confirmed. Hayden had meningitis and was in critical condition.

We spent the next two weeks in neonatal intensive care, with our newborn splayed on a platform, attached to wires and an IV. The thought that our baby could die was so unfathomable, we couldn't accept it, so we carried on as if he was just fine. Nothing antibiotics couldn't handle.

It wasn't until Hayden was no longer septic that we shed tears. The knowledge that he had survived allowed us to finally face the truth of what had just happened. The pediatrician ordered tests for Hayden's hearing in case there was residual neurological damage, but none of that mattered.

Our baby boy was alive.

When Hayden turned three, we could no longer deny the significant delays in his speech, motor skills, and cognitive skills.

"Your son has atypical autism," a developmental pediatrician at Lakenheath Royal Air Force Base in England told us. The doctor's matter-of-fact manner came across as arrogant and insensitive. I seem to remember he had his feet up on his desk, but my disdain for him may have tainted my memories.

How could he say such a thing about our tow-headed little boy, the one wearing those cute OshKosh B'gosh overalls? As the doctor dropped this bomb on our otherwise happy lives, he sat at his desk surrounded by photographs of his three apparently healthy sons playing baseball, blowing out birthday candles, and accepting citizenship awards.

What did the future hold for our son now that he was diagnosed with autism?

Francis and I were devastated. But, just like the crisis with Hayden when he was a newborn, we couldn't fathom that he would not lead a normal life. It was unthinkable; so we did every kind of therapy we could, always believing Hayden would make progress.

We found a doctor who gave us the positive outlook we were looking for and embarked on a full-time home therapy program called "floor time," along with a special diet, sensory integration therapy, speech therapy, occupational therapy, and physical therapy. It was like running a marathon—seemingly endless, exhausting work without breaks—but it was worth it because we believed there was a finish line.

Hayden progressed, sometimes painfully slowly, sometimes in exhilarating spurts. After three years of therapies, Hayden's autism diagnosis—"pervasive developmental disorder not otherwise specified"—was downgraded to a sensory regulatoi y disorder. He no longer fit the criteria for an autism spectrum disorder, but we kept going with therapy. And Hayden kept progressing, testing out of all therapies by sixth grade.

In high school, Hayden made Eagle Scout, played varsity football, was an accomplished classical pianist, starred in two theater productions, and took advanced classes. However, his lingering social delays, food and clothing sensitivities, and other idiosyncrasies made me wonder if I had been kidding myself all these years. *Would Hayden really lead a normal life or am I denying reality again?*

On a rainy day in May 2018, Hayden walked across the stage at Rensselaer Polytechnic Institute to accept his college diploma. The following Monday, he packed a lunchbox with the food he liked, put on a shirt made of fabric he found tolerable, and drove off to start his new job as a software engineer at Raytheon Company.

That was real. That was the truth. And I was happy to realize there was no denying it.

SEASON 5 ◆ EPISODE 14

THE LAST TIME

While dropping Lilly off to start her freshman year of college, I realized a certain phase of my life as a mother was coming to an end. For more than two decades, I had become accustomed to putting the needs of our three children before all else. I nurtured them as babies, guided them through their school years and multiple military moves, and saw each one of them off to college.

As I helped Lilly hang a poster in her dorm room, it occurred to me it would be the last time. The last time for all the things that have characterized an era of raising children. In an instant, my mind was flooded with an overwhelming rush of melancholy as I comprehended the end of this purpose-driven period of my existence.

This is it, I thought, *the last time...*

The last time I would hang a poster in a freshman dorm room, or fill a shower caddy with soaps and shampoos, or meet my daughter's fresh-faced resident advisor. The last time I would forget to bring a set of tools to put together the shelf unit we bought at Walmart, drop the bedrail on my foot while assembling the bed, or watch Francis standing, arms crossed, in the dorm's coed hallway shielding his baby girl from the prying eyes of her male neighbors.

The last time I would argue with my daughter over whether

or not a smoothie maker is a dorm room necessity, lecture her about boys' intentions after midnight, or explain why she needs to separate the darks from the lights when doing her laundry.

The last time I would attend a first-year parent orientation session, otherwise known as the "Free Pen Grab," embarrass my daughter by asking the campus tour guide if students are required to wear helmets when riding bikes, or wonder at the gluten-free, halal, allergy-friendly, non-genetically-modified food choices at the newfangled college dining hall.

The last time I would be duped into using a freshman orientation coupon to get a measly five percent off at the college bookstore for a fortune's worth of sweatshirts, refrigerator magnets, fleece vests, car stickers, water bottles, hats, lanyards and mousepads. The last time I would be surprised when the college staff informs me, despite the fact we are expected to pay all the bills for our child's tuition, room, board, books, WiFi, parking, health services, printing, laundry, and other undefined fees, we would never have access to her college grades, health status, or disciplinary history.

It probably wouldn't be the last time I would struggle with the thought of my innocent child being lured into one of many fraternities that line the campus, scoff at the notion she might enthusiastically engage in a game of beer pong on the red-Solo-cup-strewn fraternity house lawn, or hope and pray she wouldn't have to shower in a stall beside a football linebacker brushing his teeth in her dorm's gender-neutral bathrooms. It likely wouldn't be the last time I'd notice all the potential make-out spots along the sylvan campus paths and sigh with reluctant acceptance at the bowls of complimentary condoms scattered about the dorm common areas, health center, and student union.

But this would be the last time I'd meet my daughter in the dorm parking lot beside our minivan after freshman orientation to say farewell. The last time I would make her promise to call home every Sunday. The last time she would admit she's a little scared. The last time I would assure her the next four years would be some of the best years of her life.

And I hope, I thought as we both fought back tears, this would be the first time my daughter is the last one to let go when we hug goodbye.

SEASON 5 ◆ EPISODE 15

THE REALITIES OF NOW

Back then, I danced. I mean I *really danced.*

During my twenties and thirties, I'd hear a song that would make me spring to my feet. Channeling the beat of the music through gyrating torso and limbs, I swung my hair in loop-de-loops just for laughs. Rivulets of sweat trickled down my back, and when my evening was done, I slept like a rock.

I danced often. At cousins' weddings. On Friday nights with good friends who came over for dinner and didn't end up leaving until one in the morning. At bars or nightclubs when I was still young enough to patronize them without looking pathetic.

Now dancing just isn't the same.

For the most part, I sit and watch. But every once in a while, like an old dog who's feeling frisky, I give it a go. A really good eighties song fools me into believing I've still got it, so I shuffle to the dance floor doing a sort of pre-dance—biting my bottom lip with one fist pumping in the air—that signals everyone else to pay attention.

Once positioned I begin, but soon I realize my body doesn't dance spontaneously like it used to. I must deliberately recall the moves that used to come so freely, as I awkwardly recreate The Roger Rabbit, The Van Halen jump, and the hair swing from faded memory. Eventually, thirst and a twinge of humiliation prompt me to go back to my seat.

Later, in the wee hours, I bolt awake when my calf seizes up with cramps. And in the morning, I discover I have a kink in my neck and won't be able to turn my head to the side for four or five more days.

Back in our twenties and thirties, Francis and I were still discovering ourselves and setting standards for our life.

Perhaps we're the kind of people who brew craft beers in our garage, using interesting ingredients like apricots and toasted malts? Maybe we surf, play the harmonica in a coworker's band, bake gourmet biscotti, ride Harleys, or run marathons?

When we buy or rent a home, we will absolutely insist on stainless steel appliances. We'll use the china from our wedding registry every Thanksgiving. Romance will not be diminished when we have kids. Our children will be born using the Bradley Method, they will only eat homemade organic baby food, and will strictly adhere to a system of marble jar behavior rewards as set forth in the June issue of Parenting *magazine.*

Now, after decades of adulthood, our days of self-discovery are behind us. Life happened, and we were too busy working, paying taxes, raising kids, and keeping our marriage intact to bother with building our identity. In the process, we simply became who we are, naturally.

Our house has mismatched furniture and tumbleweeds of dog hair. I drive a minivan and take fiber supplements. Francis is bald and falls asleep in his recliner. I haven't seen our wedding china since we boxed it for storage before an overseas move more than ten years ago. The money we dreamed we might spend on exotic travel and trendy décor ended up being used on braces for our three kids, mortgages, fan belts, plumbers' bills, and college tuition. Our idea of a great Friday night is fire-pitting with the neighbors and still being in bed by 11:00 p.m.

Life isn't as we imagined it back then, but believe it or not, we're happier than we could have dreamed.

After more than two and a half decades of marriage, parenting, and military life, I may not dance all that much anymore. But I've gained the wisdom to know that, to me, it's the love of family, the companionship of friends, the honor of military life, and the richness of experience that really matter.

EPILOGUE:
IT WON'T HURT YOU, MOMMY

Somewhere in my mother's attic is a dusty blue metal canister containing an aging reel of 8mm film. I have watched it many times on our family's old projector, seeing the moving images of my childhood flashing across the screen, silent but for the rapid clicking of the ancient machine's motor. One vacation scene from this reel, taken when I was three years old, is strangely meaningful to me now that I have raised children of my own.

Bathed in the milky pastels of aging film, the shot opens on a sunny beach in North Carolina. The sky is a particular shade of blue that only seemed to exist in the 1960s, reminiscent of Melmac dishes and women's eyeshadow. The sand reflects strobing white flashes of bright sunlight. The camera pans along the shoreline, left to right, stopping when my brother comes into the picture, fifteen feet or so in the distance, splashing fearlessly in the ocean waves. Tray's flaxen crew-cut head turns—someone has instructed him to wave at the camera. His thin arm flails only for a moment, before his attention is drawn back to the bubbling surf.

Suddenly, my father's face is close in the frame, young and devoid of life's eventual complications. He is more fit than I remember, only five years outside of his college football days. My mother is the twenty-something camerawoman, capturing glimpses of her little family's day at the beach. Durwood (or "Woody" as my mother called him back then) speaks to his young wife, Diane, behind the camera, smiling and pointing to the ocean. With a jerk, the lens drops, and refocuses on my three-year-old self, clutching my father's leg.

My sandy blonde pigtails are partially covered with a blue handkerchief tied at the back of my neck, and I'm wearing a purple calico bathing suit with cotton ruffles on the top and bottom.

I hold my father's hand and smile with tiny white teeth like perfect rows of shoe-peg corn, then turn my head to gaze out at the surf. My dimpled finger points toward the water and my bright face squints up at the camera, shaking my head and clearly mouthing, "It won't hurt you, Mommy!"

I search for reassurance in my mother's eyes, and the camera bobs in affirmation. My father leads me by the hand toward the waves. As I am tugged along, I look back over my shoulder two more times to echo, "It won't hurt you, Mommy!"

We step into the surf, and I squeal and jump over foamy ripples, tightly gripping my father's hand. But suddenly, a wave rises up and takes us by surprise. My father's knees bear the brunt of its force, but I am instantly knocked into the roiling water. My father reacts quickly, plucking me, drenched and rigid, out of the surf, my mouth sucking air and my tiny hands clawing for support. Smiling, he carries me quickly toward my mother.

Just before she drops the camera to hold me, the frame captures my face, contorted in a panicked cry, reaching for the safety of my mother's arms.

The film goes on to depict shaky scenes at a petting zoo, Tray feeding a goat with a bottle, and me getting a surprise nip in the nose from a puppy. More scenes are from an afternoon barbecue outside the blue and white trailer my parents lived in while my mother was finishing her teaching degree. My father, wearing dress pants and a white shirt, turns hamburgers on a grill, while

Tray throws a football, and my grandmother Omah Jane and I spin in circles to make the skirts of our flouncy dresses take flight.

Of all these vignettes, the beach scene from our home movies was always a favorite of my brother, mother, father and me years later. As we watched together, we would all add the missing line to the silent film at the appropriate time: "It won't hurt you, Mommy!" And then we would laugh heartily at the irony of the wave knocking me down.

When my own kids were young, and I was trying to keep it all together in a world swirling with seemingly endless demands, details, and duties, I was overwhelmed. I collapsed under the weight of my perceived responsibilities as a wife and mother and felt I might be swept away.

How did I get so bogged down? What was the big deal about family rules, marble jars, and chore charts? Why did seeing another wife's gourmet cheese platter on Bunco night make me think worse of myself? What made me believe my long-standing argument with Francis about which way the toilet paper should roll could indicate we were headed for divorce? Why was I convinced that the quantity of lunchmeat I put on my kids' sandwiches directly correlated to their ability to avoid lives of crime and delinquency?

What is wrong with me? I wondered countless times.

Now I know: I was simply afraid.

Afraid of not living up to expectations. Afraid of not being smart enough, cool enough. Afraid of letting people down. Afraid of being revealed as a fraud. Afraid of not being loved. Afraid of failure.

Afraid of not being Supermom.

Fear was the underlying emotion behind every moment in which I found myself overwhelmed as a child, adolescent, young adult, wife, and mother. My over-connected, over-informed, over-competitive modern life threatened to hold me under and made me feel like I was drowning, unable to catch my breath.

I could no longer reach for the safety of my mother's arms. I had to find my own lifeline. I had to make my way through the confusing chaos of daily life, taking hold of what I valued most and wanted for myself and my family: responsibility, character, kindness, and love. The things that would lead me to solid ground.

Thanks to the yellow legal pad I carried with me to my kids' swim lessons, writing helped me find my own answers and the reassurance that everything was okay. With my focus on what was truly important, I could look back and laugh at myself and the meaningless minutiae I tried so desperately and unsuccessfully to manage. What became a weekly exercise for me as a columnist also gave me the mental clarity to carry on, day after day, month after month, year after year through the stages of family life.

And more stages are to come. Still a wife and mother, I'm negotiating the unfamiliar spaces of our now-empty nest and watching our grown children from a distance. There will surely be midlife crises of various sizes, financial worries, career stresses, weird growths, gray roots, and all sorts of marital annoyances to pick apart. The coming years will bring extended-family milestones like crying tears of joy at college graduations (if Lilly passes Organic Chemistry), bonding with future in-laws at engagement parties (as long as they know, we get them for Thanksgiving), dancing at wedding receptions (if Francis's sciatica isn't acting up), taking the grandchildren out for ice cream (as long as they follow "The Rules"), and big family vacations to Fiji paid for by our wildly-successful children (I like to think positively).

I look out at what lies ahead, and I sense the familiar mix of excitement and fear I felt at age three on the beach, standing before the great, big ocean. But now, I take in the chaos and the joy around me and remind myself with confidence, "It won't hurt you, Mommy."

CREDITS

The Husband: Francis

As readers have surely come to understand, you, Francis, are probably reading these acknowledgments hoping and expecting to see your name displayed prominently. Your inflated ego is part of what I (and many others) love about you, but your endearing self-centeredness also provided useful fodder for your character portrayal in these episodes.

So, first and foremost, I must thank you, Francis. Without you, I wouldn't have such good material. But also, you have been there, supporting me, reading with me, laughing with me, from the first essays I wrote while you were on deployment, to the public humiliation of me having your toenail described as a "little hoof" in *The Washington Post*, to the development of my blog and column, to the nights when I hadn't cooked you dinner because I was on deadline, to the times that I read my drafts to you over the phone while you were commuting from New Jersey, to the joy we both felt when I signed the contract to publish this book.

If I had a quarter for every time you bragged, "Have you met my wife, Lisa? She's a columnist, and she's written a book," we'd have enough for to pay those tuition bills. Well, not exactly, but the point is that I am forever grateful for your love and support throughout this project. You're my Day One, Honey.

The Mother: Mom, a.k.a., Maz

Because of your unconditional love and encouragement, I've read my stories to you over the telephone every week for years. You're the person I turned to for suggesting the perfect wording for a sentence, brainstorming titles, coming up with synonyms, and creative turns of phrase.

And in return for that loyalty, I offered nothing but sarcastic retorts and blatant disrespect.

Mom, thank you for never complaining when I demanded your ideas then immediately shot them down in disgust. Thanks for always answering my requests for clever words, puns, and alliterations, only to have me patently reject them. I'm grateful for the many times you suggested other options, even though I summarily waved each one off. You were the best sounding board any author could ask for.

(Truth be told, I used a lot of your ideas, and even when I didn't, our weekly calls always made my writing better.)

Love you, Mom.

The Kids: Hayden, Anna, and Lilly

If you are reading this, you must be middle-aged by now, and you found this book while cleaning out the house after I died. Don't worry, I'm not angry about that. I understand why you were never particularly interested in reading my columns and stories. For you, this was simply your life. You didn't need to read about it to know what happened.

But still, I hope this book serves as a written scrapbook of the hilarious, scary, heart-warming, sad, boring, poignant, and real moments in our family life. I was so proud to describe each one of you in this book, because being the mother of three unique, smart, loving, funny, successful, talented, compassionate children has been my greatest accomplishment in life.

Thank you, Hayden, Anna, and Lilly, for making me the

luckiest mom in the world. I love you forever.

By the way, when you come across my vintage apron collection, don't give it to Goodwill. It must be worth some money by now, so sell it on eBay, and take yourselves out to dinner together on me. XOXO

Location Manager: US Navy

This book would not exist if I were not a military spouse. Instead, I would probably be sitting in the plush corner office of my own law firm, counting my bags of money. But in a random twist of fate, I married a navy man. The navy moved us to foreign lands, rendered my law career impossible, convinced me to be a stay-at-home mom, and brought me to the brink of insanity during a year-long deployment. Without that turn of events, I would not have started writing to relieve my stress.

So thank you, US Navy, for inspiring me to write for survival, obviating the need for me to count any bags of money. In all seriousness, I consider being a military spouse an honor and a privilege. Frankly, I'm downright sappy about it. I wouldn't change my husband's twenty-eight years of service for the world. Our experiences as a military family made us richer and more grateful than we'd ever dreamed.

Thank you for the privilege of serving this country.

The Backstage Crew: Newport Round Table

When I joined our small local writer's group back in 2013, I thought you all looked like you might be serial killers. But thankfully, on that first night when my "fight or flight" instinct told me to run for the door, I resisted the urge, and instead of bolting, I wrote funny things about each of you in my notebook. Yes, I still have that notebook, and no, you can't read it.

I soon came to realize that you were all talented writers, skilled critics, and really cool characters, and that I needed your guidance. You faithfully read and critiqued my stories over and over, one after the other, until my manuscript was done. Sure, there was some drama along the way, but I cherished every moment when my readings made you laugh.

Thank you most especially to Nancy, Carolyn, and Devin. You gave me advice, encouragement, confidence, true friendship, and plenty of damned good guacamole.

The Producers: Terri and Karen at Elva Resa Publishing

If it weren't for you, Terri Barnes, I'd probably be working the night shift at 7-Eleven. We met in a mall food court when we were both stationed in Germany, launching the Patch Barracks writers group. You opened doors of opportunity to me and recommended me to replace you after you completed your tour of duty as a columnist for *Stars and Stripes*. You've been a mentor to me, so it seems perfectly scripted that you became the editor of this book.

Thank you for encouraging me to take my book idea to Elva Resa Publishing and for introducing me to Karen Pavlicin-Fragnito, publisher at Elva Resa and a fellow military spouse.

Karen, thank you for publishing my story. I couldn't be happier to work with a company dedicated to books by, for, and about military-connected folks. You are my people.

Thank you, Terri and Karen, for this opportunity, for shaping and publishing this book, of which I will be forever proud.

READER DISCUSSION QUESTIONS

In this book, author Lisa Smith Molinari is open about her own struggle to cope with the complications of parenting and marriage. In what ways can you relate to her struggle?

What aspects of the author's stories resonated with you the most? Why?

Which story in the book did you think was the funniest? Which story was the most poignant?

As Lisa discovered, sometimes the reality of marriage was different from her expectations. Have you found that to be true as well? If so, what does that mean for your relationship with your spouse? How do you address the differences between expectation and reality?

How is family life different for you than it was for your parents? How are your daily demands different from those of your parents?

Has technology had a negative or positive impact on parenting and marriage today? What are some examples from your experience?

Do you think the impact of the latest technology is different today than the impact of the technologies developed in other generations?

Research suggests that people today experience more anxiety and depression than those of previous generations. What aspects of modern life might contribute to this phenomenon?

Sometimes the minutiae and busyness of daily routines can overshadow the essentials of family life. Have you ever overlooked something important in your marriage or parenting experience while focusing on daily duties? What are your biggest distractions and how do they impact you?

In what ways did having a child with special needs affect Lisa's career path and choices? Her parenting philosophy? How were other members of the family affected?

How does humor help Lisa cope with the daily challenges she writes about? When is humor effective in mitigating family tension and stress? Are there times when humor is not effective, in your experience?

What are some other strategies families can use to cope with daily and ongoing pressures and stresses? What works best for your family?

The episodes in this book span about twenty years in the life of Lisa's family. How did her perspective change as the book progressed from her wedding to empty nest? How has your perspective changed during your years of marriage and/or parenting?

What struggles does Lisa present in "The Rise and Fall of Supermom"? How does she revisit those struggles in the epilogue, "It Won't Hurt You, Mommy"? For each, has she solved the problem or overcome that struggle? Why or why not?

How do you look for and discover the hidden meaning in the chaos of daily family life? What are the meat and potatoes of your life?